9//l

Lose that *Mommy* Guilt

Tales and Tips
From an Imperfect Mom

By

Cara Maksimow, LCSW, CPC

D1605857

An Imprint of

Open Door Publications

Lose That Mommy Guilt:
Tales and Tips From an Imperfect Mom
By Cara Maksimow, LCSW, CPC

Copyright © 2015 by Cara Maksimow
ISBN: 978-0-9960985-8-8
All rights reserved.
Printed in the United States

Cover Design by Sandy Gans, www.SandyToesCreative.com
Interior Ilustrations by Leena Thakar-Bagawde, www.shravaniarts.com

Published by
ODP Kids Books an imprint of
Open Door Publications
2113 Stackhouse Dr.
Yardley, PA 19067
www.OpenDoorPublications.com

This book has been written and published as entertainment. The author's intent is to provide information to new moms and dads through the sharing of the author's stories. These stories and opinions come from personal experiences, not from any clinical studies or therapeutic interventions.

Although the author is a practicing therapist, this book is based on her personal experiences. It is not intended and should not be used as a substitute for consultation with a physician, therapist or other health care professional. The reader is urged to be aware of their health status and to consult a medical professional in matters relating to health, exercise, diet, breast feeding, vaccines, allergies, emotional well-being or any other topic discussed in this book.

Thank you to my loving husband and amazing children for your love and support each and every day!

Table of Contents

Breathe: You Got This!

So this is it. You are about to have a baby. You have visions of being the perfect mommy with the perfect family. You dream about how you are going to do everything right, starting today. You have waited for this moment, and you have a plan.

Then reality sets in.

This is not as easy as it looks. How come other moms seem to have it all together and you are lucky if you can accomplish taking a shower today? That's mommy guilt. We all have it. It creeps in as early as pregnancy, from the moment you find out you are expecting and you think, "Oh shit, I was drinking when I did not know I was pregnant. I have already failed and I am only a few weeks along."

As the baby grows, the mommy guilt grows. It doesn't matter how good of a mom you are, you will find a way to beat yourself up over something.

I am here to say that it does not have to be that way. As moms, we are amazing and we don't recognize it enough. The next time you find yourself in an emotional place, and the mommy guilt starts to grow—stop and breathe. Remind yourself that you can do this. It will be okay.

All moms feel mom guilt, some more than others. We all want to be perfect. Guess what—you will be far from perfect—and that's okay. You got this. You do not need to let "perfect" get in the way of amazing parenting.

Recently I was invited to a string of baby showers, and it seemed that at each one I was asked what advice I would give to a first time parent. My first thought was: You will most likely fuck up every day. Welcome to the club, your baby will be fine!

> As the baby grows the mommy guilt grows. It doesn't matter how good of a mom you are, you will find a way to beat yourself up over something.

We put so much stress on ourselves to do everything right, but what does that mean? My experience has taught me that there is no such thing as doing everything right; it just comes down to taking it one day at a time, and doing the best you can.

When we expect perfection and fall short we start the pattern of mommy guilt. That guilt can grow and take over until it ultimately impacts everyone around us.

This book was written to remind all of the moms out there who have mommy guilt that they do not need to let it take over their lives. There is no such thing as perfect parenting. The more you believe YOU GOT THIS, and you let yourself off the hook for imperfections in parenting, the better off you and your family will be.

This book will take you through lessons I learned from pregnancy through grade school. I hope to provide you with engaging stories that can allow you to understand that no matter how nervous you feel about parenting, it will be okay. YOU GOT THIS. There is no single right or wrong way to do things, and above all understand that most moms want to be perfect but none of us are. The more we accept who we are and focus on our strengths and not beat ourselves up for our imperfections, the happier we will be.

I am a wife, a coach, a clinical therapist, a mentor, an

author, a public speaker, and *most importantly an imperfect mom* who has decided not to let mommy guilt get the best of me!

Here are the lessons I have learned over the years.

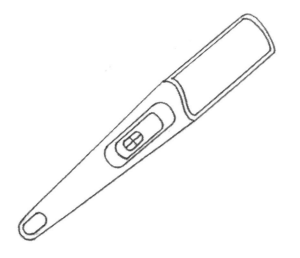

Pregnancy:
Is This Really Happening

As soon as I learned that I was pregnant, I bought and I read all the pregnancy books I could find—and still, I really had no idea what I was in for. Ten years later it seems like a big blur.

Having already had an eleven-year history, prior to pregnancy, with chronic inflammation, did not make it easier. Nothing I ate stayed in. I had morning sickness daily. How could I throw up just about every day and still put on weight? Somehow I made that happen! Some women never feel sick and ease through the first trimester. That was not my experience. The anxiety that came along with trying to take care of myself and this growing creature inside me came to be overwhelming.

One of my most memorable moments was on vacation in Cozumel. My husband and I were ten weeks pregnant with baby number one. Well, I was ten weeks pregnant— he was just along for the ride. We had originally booked the trip as a romantic vacation in order to try to get pregnant, but things didn't work out that way. I was in that "everything makes me puke" stage. Instead of a romantic getaway, ten weeks was just the right time to feel sick, feel fat, not be able to drink alcohol, but still not look obviously pregnant. I'm not sure I could have planned worse timing if

I had tried. One day during the trip we decided to take a ferry and then a two-hour bus ride to see the sights. Not sure what we were thinking!

I began to feel sick on the ferry. Imagine a boat full of people enjoying a beautiful sunny day on the water. Tourists from all over the world are laughing and smiling as I run frantically past them to get to the water to vomit. Unfortunately I did not make it to the edge of the boat. I made it half-way up the stairs, A boat employee stood at the bottom of the stairs in horror as I turned around and managed to get vomit on everything and EVERYONE nearby. Talk about a fun rest of the trip! Hot crowded bus, cranky people and the smell of vomit don't make for a great day. I almost wound up in a fist fight with a woman on the bus because she objected to me leaning my seat back a whole inch into her space. I do not consider myself a violent person, however I must admit I was ready to battle anyone and everyone who got in my way that day. I am very grateful for my 6'3" husband's ability to de-escalate the situation by just leaning forward. Heat, throw up, long bus rides, and pregnancy hormones clearly affected my ability to play well with others that day!

Once we returned from that exciting day of exploration we came back to the hotel where, again, I could not drink alcohol and had to watch everything I ate for fear of getting sick. I lived off cooked rice and the crackers I had packed in my suitcase. My husband, on the other hand, ate everything. Sure enough, he wound up bedridden with a 102-degree fever and a gastrointestinal issue. Luckily the hotel connected us to a local doctor who spoke English. The only catch was he only took cash payment, which we did not have. I wound up getting into the physician's car to drive outside the resort in search of an ATM. Looking back on the situation, it amazes me that I did not have any cash at all on hand. Even more incredible is that a nice hotel and resort had no ATM or way to access American dollars. Not the best or brightest planning, for sure! The decision to get into the doctor's car alone to leave the resort and search for an ATM was also pretty foolish, yet there I was. If I remember correctly I was so nervous that after taking out cash I left my card in the machine, only to realize it after arriving back in New Jersey.

It just so happened that the Dallas Cowboy Cheerleaders were doing a photo shoot at the same hotel the week we were there. My husband swears he is not smart enough to have planned it that way, but I still wonder. One day at the pool he tried to strike up a football conversation with some of the girls. Picture a group of beautiful young professional cheerleaders hanging out by the pool wearing bikinis, when a 31-year-old, 290-pound man with a silly vacation mustache attempts to awkwardly strike up a conversation about football. As handsome as my husband is, the "vacation stash" is not a good look. A few rolled their eyes, but a couple of them humored him for a few minutes. I laugh because he must have seemed like a creepy old man—but that did not stop him. In the hopes that he would say something sweet and reassuring, I let him know that I wasn't feeling very good about myself hanging at the pool with all the bikini-wearing cheerleaders. Nope. His response: "Honey what are you worried about, you are pregnant and you are much older than those girls." Way to go babe.

> Feeling "not ready" is natural. When you need to be ready, you will be!

I started my first pregnancy as a vegan. I hadn't eaten meat or dairy products for three years. That created a big surge of the mommy guilt. Was I doing the right thing by not eating meat or dairy? How would my diet affect the baby? All of a sudden my choices were not just about me. The pressure of making what I thought was the "right choice" wasn't easy. I could not keep any food down. Nothing. Morning sickness was a daily event, and to add to the misery, my gastrointestinal issues were not limited to morning sickness. My OB/GYN and Gastroenterologist were on my speed dial. Thankfully, with a medication change and passing time I was able to feel better. At that point my OB/GYN told me that many vegetarian and vegan women have healthy babies, however it might be time for me to eat whatever I could keep down, no matter what it was. That was the end of my meat- and dairy-free diet, and the rekindling of my love for cheeseburgers. It wasn't a surprise that my weight gain kicked in quickly from that point forward.

Gaining too much weight during pregnancy can lead to long term health risks for you and your baby. As aware of that as I was, I still gained over 60 pounds with each child. It was an absolute mommy guilt moment the day I asked my doctor, half-way through my second pregnancy, if he thought I would be able to stay under 200 pounds with this pregnancy. "Not a chance in hell," he replied.

I kept thinking, "What happened to my plan to gain thirty to thirty-five pounds and be back in my skinny jeans by the end of maternity leave?" Definitely not an option. It was a relief (and a surprise) to have passed my glucose test. Despite passing the sugar test, I knew in my heart that too much weight gain was not healthy for the baby. I beat myself up for choices I made and how much weight I gained.

My lesson here is to be proactive, not reactive. You cannot undo what is, but you can make healthier choices moving forward. Do what you can to make healthy choices, and listen to your doctor. Beating yourself up over an eleven pound weight gain in one month (yes I did that—with both kids) won't help. Accept it for what it is, and use that information to motivate you for a better month next time.

Complications may come up and you will find yourself with surprises, good and bad, throughout your pregnancy. Know that you can only control so much, and that with each unexpected thing that pops up you can absolutely handle it. Have a doctor you trust, and do yourself a favor: NEVER Google your symptoms—especially in this time of smartphones and accessibility of information. I had to go to my computer to look up strange symptoms I was feelings in order to start to panic unnecessarily. Today you can do it anywhere, anytime. Don't do it, it will only make things worse.

So enjoy the ride, embrace the heartburn, stretch marks, flatulence, crazy dreams, hiccups, and other bizarre bodily changes with the idea that this shall pass soon enough and you and the baby will be fine!

Pregnancy is a time when it can be really easy to panic and obsess over the process. Every change or movement (or lack of movement) can be worrisome. I remember many days at work thinking that I had not felt movement in a few hours and the anxiety would set in. I would poke at my belly and try to get the baby to move or wake up just so I would know he or she was still alive. When I think back to the amount of worrying and stress, I created by my own negative thoughts, it is exhausting. I realize it can be challenging, but be aware you can stop the cycle and relax. Know that you will make mistakes when you are pregnant and that will continue to be the case as a mom.

When I was pregnant with my second baby I was eating a turkey sub at work with a colleague. She mentioned her had doctor told her to never eat cold cuts when pregnant. I knew to avoid sushi and soft cheese, but turkey? I had no idea. I played it off at the time and went home to look up the risk factors of cold cuts and pregnancy. Panic was an understatement! Although the risk of infection was low, the consequences could have been awful. Once I knew and I was able to speak with my doctor about it, she reassured me everything was fine and now that I was aware it would not happen again. Accept mistakes and learn from them without feeding into the mommy guilt.

Another valuable thing I learned during pregnancy was that it is nine months for a good reason. Not just for the baby to develop, but for mom to become emotionally ready, too. A close friend was about five months along when I got pregnant. When her baby kicked, she asked if I wanted to feel it. No way! I was so weirded out. I could not imagine myself five months from the point I was at. Later, when her son was born and I visited with them, she asked if I wanted to hold him. Yeah, NO! I was not interested in going near him. I wasn't ready to hold a baby. I was about to have one of my own, but the idea of picking up my friend's baby sent panic right through me. By the time I delivered my daughter I was ready, but I needed every second up to that point, and there was no reason to feel guilty for not being ready before I needed to be.

The feeling of not being ready is natural and may not go away when the baby comes. When home with my first newborn I was visited by a friend and her one-year-old toddler. I sat with my newborn on my lap as I watched this toddler tear up toys and open and close the glass cabinet and make a mess. All I kept thinking was, "Holy shit, this little baby is going to eventually do stuff! OMG." It was chaos and I was so not ready for it. But like every other stage up until that point and beyond, when she got there, I *was* ready.

Enjoy the stage you are in and don't panic. When the time comes you will be fine at every stage, even if you do not see it now. Remember to enjoy the good parts and know the miserable parts will not last forever! Take care of yourself first because soon that will be much harder to do!

Breastfeeding:
Bigger Isn't Always Better

Everything I read or saw told me nursing was the best thing I could do for my baby's health. I went into the hospital with my first child with cards made up for the crib to be sure no one gave my baby a bottle. It was going to be only boobs. I was determined.

How wrong I was…

I want to tell you that nursing is a very personal decision. I believe that there is no right or wrong answer. Some women take to it with no problems, others struggle. Some decide not to try and others nurse until babies are really not babies any longer. It is all good. You need to find what works for you and do not let ANYONE make you feel bad for your choice, no matter what that choice may be.

I wanted to nurse. I failed miserably. …

Despite the pain when she latched on, I did not want to give up. I hired a lactation consultant to help me out. Even with her help I was not very successful. When I first brought her home from the hospital I noticed something just wasn't right. Every time she cried the hairs on the back of my neck stood up. My dad, mom, and husband all kept saying to me, "You're a mom now and babies cry, get used to it." I knew that something was off, but I just could not put my finger on it. No one believed me at first, but then I noticed crystalized urine in her diaper and I called the doctor immediately. He asked me a bunch of questions and was able to diagnose dehydration over the phone. We were told to give her formula, and within a few hours she seemed to improve. The doctor was wonderful and checked in with us every few hours for the next couple of days until we had our first visit. I was also able to go back and attempt nursing once again.

It worked and she was getting milk, however I was still miserable. I cringed every time I fed her. It hurt a lot. I consider myself good at handling pain, after all I had just given birth! How could I not handle a tiny little toothless baby? Breast feeding is one of the most natural and instinctive things a woman can do, right? Not for me. I had failed. The first big task of motherhood, and I had failed. My guilt was overwhelming. It spiraled around in my head and brought up all my doubts and insecurities about motherhood. My family tried to be supportive, and kept encouraging me to keep going despite the challenges.

> Nursing may not be right for everyone. You will choose what is best for you and your baby.

Three weeks into maternity leave I realized I was not bonding or enjoying time with my baby and I would have to go back to work soon. I kept imagining myself never feeling happy holding or caring for her. It was an awful feeling that no one seemed to understand. I struggled with the decision to stop nursing. I thought that if I stopped I would be denying her the best nutrition possible, however I could not bear to keep going. I finally decided to stop nursing and weaned her off one feeding a day for the next week. It made all the difference. I was more confident, relaxed, and enjoyed my time with her so much more. At first I felt overwhelmed and had horrible mommy guilt. I thought I had failed at the first and most basic and natural thing a mom can do. It took a few days to come to a place of peace and acceptance with my decision. I stopped focusing on the negative, went with my instincts, and looked to the benefits my choice brought. Stopping nursing let me to feel connected and bonded with my daughter as I held her and fed her with a bottle. I enjoyed our time together. I had missed this joy during the first few weeks, and I was grateful to have moved past the guilt brought on by what other people thought was best for us.

When it was time for baby number two I thought it would be different. Within hours of his birth I realized—nope—no different. I went to the first pediatrician visit when he was a couple of days old and spoke with my doctor. He was blunt and said I was just too big for the baby to properly latch onto. Nursing is not natural for everyone, and that's okay with me. I chose at that time to pump as much as I could. At first I was making lots of milk, it actually shocked me how much I could produce. Unfortunately I was trying to take care of a three-year-old, buy, and furnish a new house, bottle feed a newborn, and pump several times a day. In a short amount of time I ran out of milk. It is what it is. He was healthy and happy that was all that mattered to me.

Although nursing was not successful for me, I know many women who had wonderful experiences and missed it when their children quit. They describe feeding their babies as the best and favorite time with their children.

I believe I did what was best for both of my kids. Every mom is different; every baby is different Whatever you decide, it will be what is best for you and your child. Feel secure in your decision. Being happy and confident is more important for you and baby than whether you nurse or not.

Perfect Balance: NOT

Balance is one of those overused words that I believe can be next to impossible to achieve. Balance implies all things are neatly in line and flowing together nicely. I think of images of ballerinas posing perfectly on toes with hands in the air. In my world it is more like a seesaw constantly in motion as I try to avoid dropping balls flying out of control over my head. That is the way it is for most moms from what I can see.

I don't believe there is ever perfect balance. The highly charged conversation on working moms has created quite a debate. Can women have it all? Some say yes, some say no, and others say not all at once. I have to say it all depends on how you define ALL. What it means to have it all is subjective for so many women, and it also may change over time.

Rising on the corporate ladder requires moms to spend less time at home. Spending more time at home usually requires putting careers on a slower pace or on pause for some time. For some families, mom has a high-level career and dad (or partner) has flexible hours, stays home, or works part-time. Other families have strong nannies or extended family to help with the care of the children. Some use day care centers. Often there is not much of a choice involved. Two working parents are essential in so many households, so finding that right balance, as difficult as it is, is something to continually strive for. There is no right or wrong answer. No matter how much time you have with your kids, understand that it is more important to make the most of the time you have than to beat yourself up over the time you don't have.

I left a social work job where I worked very long hours and had high level of responsibility as the director of a thirty-bed psychiatric facility to be a pharmaceutical sales rep so that I could have better hours for raising a family. By the time I started having kids I was a regional trainer and was traveling quite a bit.

When I took what I thought would be a family-friendly job I did not consider my competitive drive and desire to be constantly challenged. This meant I moved into more challenging positions. As a trainer I needed to be out of the state my second week back from maternity leave. I was not ready to get on an airplane and fly hours away from my baby for an entire week. I was barely ready to drop her at day care to go to work each day.

The panic set in as I planned my return to work. Could I leave her for that long? Even if I could, I knew my husband was not ready to be on his own with her, either. The obvious option was to not go on the trip. After all, just returning from family leave it would be reasonable to delay travel, right?

Then came the guilt. This time the mommy guilt was about my career. The competitive side of myself did not want to be seen as uncommitted to my career now that I was a mom. At the time I did not believe I had a choice, so I took her with me! Looking back on it now, I am not really sure if I would do it the same way again. However it was what it was.

My company offered "back up" daycare in specific centers around the country. After much research and second guessing myself, I chose to take her with me on the trip. She flew on my lap and stayed in the hotel with me, even attending dinner or evening events. She went to the "back up" day care center a few miles from where I was working and I was able to be with her all evening and night.

I did this quite a few times for the first few months back to work. I made it work. I had a system for packing toys, alcohol wipes, and powdered formula. It was a blessing to have her with me when I traveled. I was determined to "get it right" and did not want my dedication to be questioned just because I was a new mom. Although it worked out well, in hindsight I probably could have backed down from a few of those travel trips and it would have been okay. As time went on, taking her with me got tougher.

> The competitive side of myself did not want to be seen as not committed to my career now that I was a mom.

When my daughter was not able to be contained in the hotel crib for very long, I knew I needed to have her stay home with her daddy, or move into a job with considerably less travel.

A local District Manager position opened up and I will always remember how desperately I wanted to move from a role with high travel to a local leadership role. During the interview, the hiring VP said that he was not sure what to do because he wanted to have me as a member of his management team, but he did not think that if I was given the job I would stay in it long-term. If caught between my job and my family, my family would win out. He was right. So now what?

I knew my current job had too much travel, however the management position I was interviewing for was not really much better. I was living in New Jersey and the opening I was interviewing for was in Brooklyn. Looking back I realize that daily commute would have most likely put me over my tipping point.

I was very fortunate to have support from senior management and I wound up being offered a management position in New York City. The position was part-time, managing a smaller sales team. Although I still traveled, it was minimized by the fact that I worked a three-day work week.

> Another lesson I leanred when I ws working part-time was to be present in the moment, whatever you are doing.

After a few years, the part-time postion was no longer available. However, by then I was experienced enough in the job that when I was asked to go back to full-time I negotiated for flexibility. I took on a full-time position, but worked four days a week at eighty percent compensation. It was a fantastic solution at the time.

Another key factor to consider when trying to balance career and family is a back up plan. Having back up babysitting options can make a huge impact on career decisions. Unexpected circumstances will happen.

I remember when I was pregnant with my son and I was working as a sales manager in New York City and my meeting uptown ran later than expected. I knew exactly what time I needed to get to my car and be in the Holland Tunnel traffic in order to get back to the day care to get my daughter on time. That particular day I did not make it. The traffic was just awful. I was only a few miles from home when the tunnel was backed up; those few miles could take hours. Sure enough that day it happened.

As I sat in traffic I could feel the tension, anxiety, and guilt build as I realized I was not going to get to the day care center before closing. Thankfully, I had a cell phone and could call and check in with the teachers. I tried to get my husband, but he was also stuck in meetings in Midtown. Being pregnant and in need of a bathroom did not make it any easier.

I checked in with the school every half hour or so, and eventually convinced one of the teachers to walk my three-year-old home to our building, get the key from the doorman, and make dinner. Thankfully, it worked out and I managed to get home about two hours after the school was closed.

I felt so guilty, assuming my daughter would feel abandoned. Nope, not at all. The guilt was all mine. She loved her teacher and was thrilled to have her take care of her. The teacher also made some extra cash and then became one of our go-to sitters. It all worked out fine and I learned to always have a back-up plan. Looking back on that incident, I realize that my assumptions about what my daughter was feeling created an avalanche of anxiety and guilt when in reality she was thrilled.

Another lesson I learned when I was working part-time and raising my kids was to be present in the moment, whatever you are doing. I had so many times at work when I felt guilty and missed my babies, and other times when I was with the kids taking work calls and stressing over something going on at work, and was not present in the moment for them.

You would be shocked how much wasted time can be

spent when you your head is elsewhere. Don't get me wrong, I have not yet mastered being present. The urge to check emails or take work related calls during my child's softball game or family time still happens. I just try to give in less often.

It took me a while to get that message, and I know that when I was working long hours I was not always my best as a mom, and not always my best as a Sales Manager. I remember a big "aha" moment when I was preparing my team for my second maternity leave. I was meeting with my boss and going over my coverage plan for my maternity leave. I want to preface this story with the fact that he was a tough boss and "all business." I would normally walk out of performance reviews feeling as if I was hit by a Mack Truck. He had high expectations and did not allow me to bullshit my way through anything. I had a healthy fear and respect for his leadership.

During that particular meeting I was stressing over plans for the launch of a new product. I wanted to be sure my team didn't drop the ball and that every detail was covered during the few months I would be away. Perfectionism was rearing its ugly head. I wanted to ensure success for my team while I was gone. That is when my boss gave me advice I will never forget.

"Plan the best you can, but when the time comes to have the baby, let everything at work be." He said that he had four kids and he remembered the birth of each one of his children as if it were yesterday. "If anyone were to ask me what was going on in my career at the time my kids were born I could not tell you," he said.

I have always remembered his advice. It put things into perspective for me, particularly because he was one of the toughest and most driven leaders I had ever worked for.

My flexible work hours made a big difference in my ability to take care of my family for many years. I am not saying this is an option for everyone, but I would have never had the chance had I not asked for it. I learned that just because something was not done that way before does not mean it can't be. It does not hurt to ask. Do your research and go in prepared when asking for outside the box arrangements. You may be surprised what is possible.

Despite having one day off a week, I still missed a lot of things at school and I found myself more stressed than I thought that I should be. I realize now that so much of the stress came from the darn mommy guilt.

A few years ago I left my sales job to start my own business so I could be more available to my family. Even now that I make my own schedule around my children's schedules, I sometimes have a conflict with an event at school that I can not change.

My husband is often traveling as well. It is not perfect, but we find a way to make it work. I have found little rituals can help provide comfort to you and your little one when you need to be away more than you would like.

Having back up babysitting options can make a huge impact on career decisions. Unexpected circumstances will happen.

For example, when I would leave for a trip or even leave for a long day at work I would draw a heart on my kids' hands and they would do the same to me. We then blow kisses and catch them with the heart. Throughout the day my kids and I can look at the heart and be reminded of each other.

For school events and activities, I am very fortunate to

have extended family living locally, and a grandma and grandpa who can go in my place. Despite my initial guilt over not being there for everything, my children are thrilled to have their grandparents come instead.

When I think about those situations, I remember a time when I was a child in grammar school and I had won the student of the month award. I was called up on stage in front of the entire school to get my certificate. It was a big deal for a small kid. Each month one student got this award and often parents came to the assembly to see their child receive it. The day I went on stage, my parents both had to work.

As I walked off the stage and back to my seat my teacher handed me an envelope. It was a note my mother had written and asked the teacher to give me. She wrote how proud she was of my achievement and how much she and my father loved me. As much as I wanted them there, I fondly remember that note thirty-five years later. Now, as I am a mom, I imagine my parents wanted very much to be there and most likely felt guilty they could not attend, yet I have only positive memories of that day.

Do I think it is possible to have it all? The lesson I learned is that this is a very subjective question and it depends on how you define it. I define having it all as raising happy, healthy, resilient kids while still doing what I enjoy. I set an example for my children by being forgiving of others and of my own imperfections.

Whether you are working full-time, part-time, or are home, accepting what you have and being present in the moment will go a long way to warding off mommy guilt. It is not about how much time you have, but what you do

I define "having it all" as raising happy, healthy, resilient kids while still doing what I enjoy.

with it. That often means taking time for self-care and embracing the idea that the perfect supermom just does not exist.

Sleep: Maybe One Day

Bedtime can be the most wonderful time of the day, with cuddles and hugs and intense conversations. It can also be the most exhausting and frustrating time of the day.

Why is it that children never want to go to bed? I haven't quite figured out when children go from fighting the need for sleep to actually enjoying it. As a morning person, I turn into a pumpkin pretty early in the evening, and by the time I get my kids to bed I am long ready to go to sleep.

So when is the ideal time to put your kids to bed? It varies so much from family to family. In our house bedtime is approximately eight o'clock each evening. but I stress the word approximately. There is always procrastination and negotiation about why they should stay up. When they finally go up to get ready they take forever... and ever. They argue with each other, run around and play and ultimately someone winds up yelling or crying.

Sometimes that someone is me. One particular night the sibling rivalry started over my son stealing candy kisses from my daughter's "candy stash" in her room. Next thing I knew chaos had erupted and it took over a half an hour to stop them from yelling at each other and focus on going to bed.

It is a right of passage for kids to challenge the bedtime

routine. They want to make sure they don't miss anything. Sleep is boring to them and they really don't see why they need to go to bed if they don't want to.

I learned that bedtime routines can make a huge difference in turning bedtime from a war zone into bonding time. That does not mean that all of your children need to go to bed at exactly the same time. My older child gets a half an hour to an hour longer than her brother, however the key is that they both need to be ready for bed at the same time. If that happens, then she can stay up a little longer.

Nightmares and fears can make for challenges in tucking in. Visualization is a strategy I found can help with nightmares. When tucking the kids in I have them bring up images in their minds of a favorite place, someplace that makes them feel calm and happy and safe. I ask lots of questions to get a rich picture of this special place. Who is with them? What are they wearing? What are they seeing, smelling, feeling? What are they doing? My daughter's favorite visualization is of a beach, swinging on a swingset with mommy. We are both wearing ball gowns and sparkly shoes. It smells like flowers, the sun is shining bright and beautiful music is playing in the air (Indigo Girls—yes I taught her well). We would talk through this scene and the feeling of the ocean breeze on our faces as we swing back and forth. My daughter would then have that image in her head as I tucked her in and she went to sleep. Bringing her back to that same place each night she felt scared or clingy eased her fears and created a safe and happy place.

Monsters present a similar, but different, bedtime issue. Yep, all kids at some point or another seem to think there are monsters. A hairspray bottle labeled "Monster Repellant" sometimes works. If you have never done it, it is super easy. Just take an empty spray bottle and fill it with water and create a "Monster Repellant" label. Perhaps you will be more creative with the name. I chose the obvious, I know. Spray the bedroom with the water before bed, and explain to the kids that this is special monster repellant that will keep any monsters away.

With my little boy I needed a different approach. I would explain to him how his daddy made sure when we signed the papers to buy the house that there was a section of our contract that said it was a monster-free house. It was "guaranteed by law" and this way we could be sure that we would have no monsters. That worked like a charm.

If it wasn't monsters keeping my kids up, it was something else. As babies I must admit that thumb sucking and binkies made bedtime much easier. I know, I know, the dentist was not a fan—but with my oldest, the binky was a necessity. You will likely hear varying opinions on having binkies and stuffed toys in bed. For infants, I get it. Stuffed toys can be dangerous, however as my kids got a bit older a favorite stuffed toy and blankie were a must for bedtime routines. In fact, still is.

When it is time to put a second baby to sleep there is a toddler or older child around who is used to having mommy all to herself, and sure enough the new baby manages to fall asleep without the extra rubbing, cuddling, and rocking.

Reading books at bedtime can also be an important part of the bedtime ritual. I will be honest, I am not as good at that as I should be. When they were little, I was better. Now, not so much. When they started reading, they would read to me, but that did not last too long. Now I encourage reading each night for twenty minutes. Sometimes it happens and sometimes not. I keep trying.

Forcing them to read doesn't work in my house, but having plenty of books available and encouraging them to read leads to better habits. Seeing me reading also helps them to want to do the same. Don't stress if your child is not interested in books at some point or another, just keep many available and make it a part of the routine.

Another ritual that I have learned has some benefit is singing. You do not need to have any talent at all. Trust me on this. Anyone listening would tell you how tone deaf I am—except my children. They enjoy little songs as I kiss them goodnight. As babies I would sing A LOT. The older they get the less it happens, but when having a particularly tough night I know that if I start singing the song I sang them as babies it instantly comforts and relaxes them.

This is a good time to discuss what many people told me was one of my biggest mommy mistakes—holding my first baby every night till she fell asleep. I had read all the controversy over co-sleeping. Some say it is a wonderful bonding experience. They will tell you that a mom knows instinctively where her baby is at all times. I agree with that in theory. Then there was the other side of the argument. Safety. Babies suffocate. There are stories of moms falling asleep nursing or having too much alcohol and babies getting smothered. That scared the hell out of me, so then what was I to do?

I chose a co-sleep crib, but tried to keep her out of the bed itself when I was truly sleeping (and when my husband was home asleep as well).

After a long day of work and caring for a newborn, I found myself holding my firstborn at bedtime until she fell asleep in my arms. Then I put her in the crib while she was sleeping. I loved that time together. It was our special time, just the two of us. Maybe it was the guilt of not being with her much of the day, or just how much I missed her, but I needed that time. The difficulty came when she got a little older and I was not able to sit for the time it took for her to fall asleep. I definitely created an issue for anyone else who tried to put her down at night. My husband told me it took hours trying get her to go to sleep. Every time he put her down she would cry, and he wound up picking her up and holding her until she went to sleep, and then as soon as he put her in the crib she would cry again.

So for all you moms out there who find yourself in similar situation and now have a baby that needs you as part of the bedtime ritual, the good news is it won't last forever. I started putting her in the crib awake and rubbing her back till she fell asleep. After that started to work (and it took a week or two) I began to put her down and then sit on the floor by the crib, a few times I even ate my dinner right there on the floor. No big deal, but it required patience and consistency with the routine. That was the most important thing I learned—make sure if you start something, be consistent every day. Once you start and stop and start again you have just set yourself up for failure. (That is also something I learned about potty training as well.)

It is amazing to me how much the mommy guilt plays into bedtime for the firstborn, and yet when baby number two comes along, everything changes. When it is time to put a second baby to sleep there is a toddler or older child around who is used to having mommy all to herself, and sure enough the new baby manages to fall asleep without the extra rubbing, cuddling, and rocking. Amazing how that happens! Maybe that's why my firstborn still likes to cuddle and sleep in bed with mommy more than my second child does. Another trigger for the mommy guilt: did my son not get enough attention or did I create a stronger sense of independence in him? Probably a little bit of both.

Bedtime can also be a great time to use rewards for good behavior and encourage independence. One night a week, usually Friday, my husband and I take a night off from the bedtime ritual by allowing the kids to watch TV in our bed. If both kids go up and get ready for bed with no issues, they can go to our bedroom and watch TV until they fall asleep or until we want to go to bed. They see it as a huge treat to get to stay up and watch TV, and I see it as a night to hang out on the couch after eating pizza and not get up again for quite a while. Selfish? Maybe, but I like to see it as a win-win for all!

Colds, coughs, boogers, nightmares, sleepwalking, stomach aches, fevers... you name it, something would happen at night.

The most important bedtime ritual we started a couple of years ago has become the most consistent. We call it "B.A.G." The idea is that thoughout the day we all have obstacles and negativity that can build up and weigh us down at bedtime. Together we imagine emptying an imaginary B.A.G. of the stress and negativity out onto the floor and then fill it up with three things that spell B.A.G. B stands for the Best part of the day, A for what we Accomplished, and finally G is for Gratitude. Gratitude is a very important part of my life and my work as a therapist, therefore I want to instill it in my children. We spend a few minutes at bedtime sharing our B.A.G. A particular playdate, a safe flight home, good dinner, or a fun activity at school tend to top the list. This activity has become a standard ritual each night. The kids remind me when I forget.

You may be thinking—yeah right—some days there is nothing to be happy about. You may be right that sometimes we have really bad days. I agree, but if you are still breathing, you have at least one thing for the day. I can admit there have been a few times when I have had an unusually frustrating day and I think, "I got nothing!"

One particular day I remember my son sharing his B.A.G. and saying "Mommy, it's your turn." Ugh, can't he just go to sleep for goodness sakes? Nope. If I expect him to do it when he is cranky, then I need to do the same. That day I closed my eyes and replayed my day in my head and sure enough I came up with my B.A.G. to share with him. It does not have to be something big to be meaningul. I am truly grateful that my son pushes me to practice what I preach, even when it isn't easy.

When we think of bedtime and sleep, we often think of how important it is for our little ones and accept the fact that as parents the first thing we lose is the luxury of a full night of sleep. Sleep deprivation often starts in pregnancy. With both pregnancies I remember wondering if I would ever sleep again. While pregnant, I was constantly kept up by something. Some nights it was heartburn, others leg cramps, and others just plain discomfort. By the way, the leg cramp thing is no joke. I would wake up screaming in pain, feeling as if someone was stabbing my calf with a butcher knife. Whatever it was, it was painful!

Another pregnancy sleep-buster was hiccups: not mine, the baby's. It was so creepy. Amazing that my babies only got hiccups in the womb when I was trying to fall asleep.

As much as I waited for the baby to be born so I could sleep, I learned pretty quickly that a good full night's sleep would forever be a treat, and not a given.

Once my first child was born, I amazed myself with the fact I could function with no more than three hours of sleep at a time. I did take little naps here and there, but I longed for seven or eight straight hours. It did come eventually, but it took a few months. The best piece of advice is to sleep when the baby sleeps.

I know that can seem unrealistic. I mean, when would the house get cleaned or other things get done? Well in the very beginning—who cares? If you have help, great! If not, let the housecleaning go for a bit. It is not the end of the world if dishes pile up or the rug needs a vacuum. Get some sleep and enjoy time with this baby who is changing and growing by the second! Those early months were some of my favorite bonding times. In fact just the other day my seven-year-old boy and I napped on the couch together on a lazy rainy afternoon and it brought back such wonderful memories of those first few months.

Some nights I would get to go to sleep around eight o'clock in the evening, with the baby after feeding, then my husband would wake up and feed her between eleven o'clock and midnight before he went to bed. This way I could sleep until three in the morning, when it was time for another feeding. Having had plenty of sleep, I would sometimes enjoy that time sitting in the dark, quiet room alone with my baby. I want you to understand that some nights it all fell into place that way, other nights were just a blur of crying, feeding, and sort of sleeping.

By about four months old, both of my kids were sleeping through the night. I am aware that experience is not the case for everyone. I still got up some times around three o'clock in the morning, but it did not last that long, and was not every night. So many parents I talk to have kids who get up in the night long after four months. Often the child is not hungry, but just wants soothing. My daughter would wake and want the binky. I had about a hundred of them in her crib, so she could perhaps get lucky and grab one. Usually I was the one to go put it in her mouth throughout the night.

As they got to be toddlers, I thought I would sleep well every night, but that was just not the case. Colds, coughs, boogers, nightmares, sleepwalking, stomach aches, fevers… you name it, something would happen at night. Night terrors were the worst. My daughter would scream as if she was having a horrible nightmare, and when I would try to console her she would look through me and continue to cry. The more I tried to help, the worse it got.

That was frightening. She outgrew it eventually, but boy was that disturbing. One time she had one of those nights when I was in California for work. She was about three or four years old. I had my parents sleeping at the house to help my husband with the morning school routine. I got a phone call in the middle of the night. When I saw the incoming call from home around midnight, I panicked. What could be going on: housefire, accident, burst appendix? My mind went wild with fears as I answered the phone. My husband called to say that my daughter needed me. He put her on the phone in the midst of a night terror. Really? Are you kidding me? Three adults and you can't deal with one little girl? She cried and cried and no matter how much I told her mommy would be home, she just kept sobbing.

Cherish those solid nights of good sleep, because at every age there is some type of sleep-buster waiting to rear its head.

Eventually, after my heart was pretty much ripped out of my chest, my husband came back on the phone and said that my parents were taking her back to bed and thanks for trying. I was crushed. I spent the remainder of the night fantasizing about quitting my job and flying home first thing in the morning. I finally fell asleep, and reality set in the next day. I will always remember that horrible feeling of guilt and helplessness, and yet my daughter did not remember a thing the next day.

Our newest sleep-buster has been sleep-walking. My little boy will get up at night, wander around the house, and have no memory in the morning. He sometimes starts to cry and I wake up and try to put him back to bed. If I am quiet and just help him walk to his bed it works okay. One time he urinated on the floor of his bedroom in his sleep. He had no memory of it. Although situations like that are not common, it doesn't make them less annoying.

My son often comes into my bed looking for me. He will crawl in bed with me and my husband briefly, and then go back to bed. When he sleepwalks and I am not home or not up in my room yet, he will go to his sister's room and crawl in bed with her. They both don't realize it until I go and check on them and carry him back to his room. Neither remember it in the morning. It is such a cute sight to see. Glad to know at the subconscious level they comfort each other so well.

As the kids get older the controversy continues over whether or not to let kids in your bed. Every night I would say absolutely not, but honestly once in a while I am fine with it. I also found my son wants no part of sleeping with us. In fact I am sure it is because with him I often had to have him cry to sleep because I had a three-year-old in the bath or a fussy toddler who I was reading to. By the time I would go back to the baby, he was asleep. He now sleeps very well on his own and doesn't want to sleep with us at all. My daughter, on the other hand, wants to sleep with me any time she can.

So my big lesson is, cherish those solid nights of good sleep because at every age there is some type of sleep-buster waiting to rear its head. I am sure waiting up for teenagers when the time comes will be no exception!

Playdates:
Moms Need Them, Too

When I was a kid we just played. Not sure when that turned into a "playdate." I used to look at playdates kind of like dating for mommy more than baby. Those early months of maternity leave were like being newly single on a mission to find a mate. I was thrilled to find a flier for a group playdate for toddlers once a week in my building. I showed up with a two-week old baby the moment I was able to get myself and my newborn out of the apartment and down the elevator to the playroom. Clearly my newborn didn't benefit from that playdate—but mommy sure did! That time was particularly hard for me. My husband had gone back to work during the day and family and friends had their work and their lives. I was isolated and felt overwhelmed. Having that play group to connect to other moms made a huge difference. I met a handful of other new moms I was able to spend time with during those first few weeks.

When the family, friends, and even spouses all go back to work, real-life motherhood in those early days can be so very lonely. Hormones are still all funky and emotions run wild. That can be normal. Looking for other moms to spend time with can be an important part of the adjustment to motherhood. While pregnant, it can help to collect numbers and contacts of other pregnant new mommies in your area, perhaps at a childbirth class or maternity shopping. You can also find lots of resources on Facebook and other online sites as well. New mommy groups are everywhere, you just need to look.

Please know that there is a difference between baby blues and depression. If you are not sure how you are feeling and think you could be depressed or anxious, please do not hesitate to reach out and tell someone. Tell your spouse, friend, or a family member. Reach out for help. You are not alone. There are many therapists and organizations that specialize in postpartum depression and I urge you to reach out. There is strength in asking for help for you and your family.

> When the family, friends, and even spouses all go back to work, real-life motherhood in those early days can be so very lonely.

Often the process of finding other parents to hang out with can be compared to dating. How long do you wait to call once you meet? Do you invite your playdate group to the birthday party? Will they like you? Will the kids stay friends if the parents like each other? What if we do not like the parents of the kids our kids like? It can be exhausting!

My husband and I found in the early years that our social world revolved around the other families at day care. As time went on, we found most of the time, the parents we enjoyed spending time with were the parents of kids our kids liked to play with. It usually works out that way.

One rushed morning while walking my oldest to kindergarten she said to me, "Do you like so and so's mommy?"

"Why, yes, I do, why?"

"Okay, I am giving her your number and inviting her for pizza."

After I went to work, my daughter's friend arrived at school and she ran up to her mother and said, "Do you like my mommy, she really likes you," and handed her a note with my cell number and asked her over for pizza.

Despite the backward nines my daughter had printed on the paper, the mom figured out the phone number and called later that day. Yes, we had them over for pizza and years later all still hang out regularly.

Do not stress over not knowing enough families with kids the same age, or in same phase, as your child. You will meet them through activities and preschool. Trust the judgment of your little one. He or she will guide the way.

When our oldest was three, we moved to a town in the burbs where we did not really know anyone. Eventually, we started to meet other families as I dropped off and picked up my child at school. Be patient, and don't be afraid to initiate. The other parents most likely are also looking to meet other families, too.

One valuable lesson I learned about making playdates is to start slow. I love the idea of planning vacations with other families so that kids and grownups have someone to hang out with. But do not jump in too quickly. Think of the courting process and ease yourself into relationships. You will find lasting connections if you take your time. You may imagine that you will have babies at the same time as your friends and then raise your kids as best buddies. That is great, but not always the reality.

Boogers: And More Boogers

One of the most difficult things to deal with as a parent is to see your baby sick. Whether it is something serious, or just a little cold, it can be stressful. No matter how much you wash your hands, eat healthy, or do all the right things, children are little germ factories. Being around other babies and kids will bring on the boogers.

I learned pretty quickly that day care was a big petri dish, always some sort of runny nose going on. On those many long nights I would sit up to monitor fevers and boogers I worried that I had made the wrong choice putting her in day care. What I learned from our doctors was, although I felt awful exposing her to so many germs at such a young age, her immune system would benefit from it the same way that kids generations ago built up immunity by being in a household with many siblings and extended family members. Hearing that was helpful—although it did not take away the stress when a little one would get sick.

Is there anything that can be done to prevent illness? Keeping hands washed and staying on time with vaccinations can make a big difference. Whether or not to vaccinate is loaded topic for many parents. I must admit, even working for a pharmaceutical company and knowing the benefits of vaccines, I did not like the idea of sticking my baby with what seemed like never-ending shots. After doing my own research and reading, I am certain that vaccines save lives. The data is clear. The anti-vaccine movement began with a debunked study that has been proven to be false. The physician leading the movement has lost his license to practice medicine. Please do not take my word for it, do your own research. With full due diligence you should feel confident in your informed decision.

A vaccine available today that was not available when I had my first child is for rotavirus. Around her first birthday, the rotavirus ran through my daughter's day care class. Of the twelve babies, nine came down with the virus, and five of the nine were hospitalized. For those of you not familiar with this particular virus, it manifests as fever and diarrhea. Not good. As I said before, hand washing is crucial, and this was a clear example of lack of hand washing in the classroom.

My daughter was hospitalized after a few days of diarrhea and fever. The stress and guilt started when I took off from work to bring her to the doctor after a day or two of her having this virus. After examining her, the pediatrician told me I could not go home and that I was to drive to the hospital right from the office visit. She was dehydrated and he was concerned about that, and the risk of febrile seizures. I was terrified. I had no idea what was going to happen next.

Once we were at the hospital and admitted to a room, the stress escalated. The nurses needed to put an IV in her arm and refused to allow me in the room as they did it. The reason they provided to me was that infants tend to cry and reach for parents more when they can see mom or dad in the room, so in order to insert the needle they needed me out of the room. That was not what I wanted to hear!

The room had a glass window with blinds I could peek through if I squinted. I was able to put my head up to the glass and peer through the slates to see my one-year-old baby crying as she was held down by several healthcare workers in order to insert the needle into her hand. I had a pit in my stomach wondering if I should have demanded they let me be there for her. Would they have let me be there to help comfort her or would I have ended up being asked to leave?

Once the IV was in place, my baby hated it. She was too little to use words, but her actions were clear. She kept tugging at it and holding her hand towards me with sad little eyes. I knew she wanted me to take it off of her. I felt helpless and guilty despite knowing there wasn't anything I could do other than be there for her.

We sang, played games, and read baby books until she fell asleep. Later that night I almost wound up in an altercation with the nurses because they would not allow me to hold her as we slept. My daughter was not allowed to be on the cot with me for fear of falling off, and I was not allowed to sleep in the big metal crib because the crib was not meant to hold an adult. In other words, I was just too big. I slept in the crib anyway. I crawled in and cuddled with my girl, pulling the bar up behind my back despite the nurses' threats to have me removed. My baby needed comfort from her mommy, and frankly mommy needed it, too!

At one point in the middle of the night, I woke up wet

> Pediatricians, like anyone else, do the best they can, but do not always have the answers. If something does not feel right, trust your instincts and get another opinion.

45

and noticed her IV was leaking all over the crib. I quickly alerted the nurse, and they had to re-insert it in my daughter's hand. I am grateful I continued to disobey the staff, since that is how I found out that it was not properly inserted and she was not getting the benefit of the fluid she desperately needed. After a few days the virus ran its course and we were fine to go home. It would have been nice to have had a way to prevent that experience as there is today.

Over the years we've had a concussion, many instances of strep throat, bronchitis, bronchiolitis, and lots and lots of boogers. In the end, my biggest lesson is to not go crazy looking up symptoms on the internet. Dr. Google will do nothing but freak you out. Just make sure you find a pediatrician you like and trust (we have had quite a few), and make sure you have a number you can call any time. One of the lessons I learned is that large medical practices with multiple doctors can be good for those late night calls. They all take turns so you can usually get someone on the phone. We had a pediatrician I liked very much, but when she went on vacation she had someone covering who had his own practice.

My son was ten-months-old and had what the doctor said was bronchiolitis. It was lasting a long time. We had not been on antibiotics and he seemed to be getting worse. I called the covering doctor and left a tearful message asking him to call me back because my baby was struggling for air, and I was concerned. He never returned my call. I had an antibiotic prescription at home because my doctor given it to me in case we needed it for another illness. I started it on my own. Maybe not the best choice, but at the moment I was convinced the virus had become a bacterial infection.

I went in to my doctor a few days later, and told her the covering doctor had never returned my calls, and I started treatment on my own. I had made the right call. Shortly after that my son wound up with reactive airway disease and asthma. Because he was so young, I struggled with the decision to give medication which was not prescribed for that particular episode. However, I knew something was very wrong. At ten months old I could tell he was wheezing and struggling to breathe, despite the nebulizer treatments.

Doctors do not always have all the answers. Be patient and go for a second opinion if need be. Medicine is not always perfect and there are many options for treatment. Different doctors have different experiences, differing opinions, and will make different choices. For example, my son was not circumcised, and at a pediatrician appointment I was told that he needed to see a urologist. (He was in kindergarten at the time.)

The urologist basically said that circumcision was a must, and insinuated poor parenting on my part. Talk about feeling guilty. Here was a respected medical professional telling me I had not properly taken care of my child! He asked me why I had not been helping him pull back his foreskin. What! He was six years old and fully capable of urinating without mommy's help. At no point did I think I should be involved.

Of course, after talking with the urologist, I began second guessing myself, and thinking I had screwed up a major medical decision. My husband and I had made the decision not to circumcise based on researching pros and cons, speaking to other parents, and following the advice of our pediatricians at the time. My husband and I disagreed at first, and I convinced him with the information I gathered.

Now, years later, I was being told that I was wrong to have not circumcised him as an infant, and that I needed to schedule to have it done immediately. To make matters worse, all of this was said in front of my son. The entire ride home he cried and cried, and asked me why I didn't do it when he was a baby. OMG. I was crushed. After pulling myself together I spoke to other physicians about what happened, and made the decision to not return to the urologist and allow the natural process to work itself out. He, and his penis, are fine.

Pediatricians, like anyone else, do the best they can, but they do not always have the answers. If something does not feel right, do not hesitate to see a specialist. Even then, if you don't feel confident, seek a second opinion. Keep in mind that despite all of the education, the training, and the professionalism of many healthcare professionals, they are human.

That reminds me of a time when I brought my daughter to a dermatologist for bumps on her back. At birth, we noticed a few little bumps that looked like pebbles under her skin on her lower back. The pediatrician was concerned and asked us to keep an eye on them until she was a bit older. As a toddler, we brought her to the dermatologist to have them checked out. The dermatologist had me lie on the table in the office, and had my daughter lie on my chest as the doctor removed one of the bumps to biopsy.

My baby cried so much that the front of my shirt was soaked with tears during the few minutes it took to get the sample. The dermatologist finished and ran out of the room quickly. Two weeks later when we returned to the office to learn that the bumps were nothing to worry about the dermatologist apologized for leaving the room the day of the procedure. She explained that she, as a new mom herself, had become overwhelmed with emotion seeing how upset my daughter was with the procedure, and she had to run out of the room as to not let us see her break down and cry. She said that the numbing cream should have reduced any pain or discomfort, however based on how intensely my daughter had been crying, she feared it had not worked.

That situation shows how intense mommy guilt can be for all of us. Even a trained healthcare professional could not hold back her emotion during a pretty routine medical test when she thought she had caused someone else's little girl to cry.

Another person who can be a really great source of support and information when it comes to the health of our children is the school nurse. They are acutely aware of developmental milestones, and have a good sense of what is usual and what is not for school-age children. They see it all day long. Based on a school nurse alerting me to bloody noses that seemed more frequent than the average, I took my kids for bloodwork. According to the nurse, the bloody noses were harder to get under control than she was used to seeing, and she suggested I check it out.

Since birth, both of my kids would get petechia (broken capillary blood vessels) and doctors repeatedly told me it was not a big deal. Add the bloody noses to the mix, and the results of blood work, and even the pediatrician raised an eyebrow. We saw a hematologist, and after a scare with the first blood test, we found the first test was inaccurate. The hematologist explained to me that the blood most likely sat for too long in the lab before it was tested. A second test showed that everything was fine, and a minor issue was addressed. The results of the original bloodwork had given us a false positive. This reaffirmed the need for parents to do proper due diligence and seek another opinion.

Keep in mind that as a new parent, your kids will bring germs into the house you may not be immune to. A little tummy trouble for one of the kids usually sends my husband to the latrine for at least twenty-four hours. Never fails. Once we had a party in our home when my little one was a baby. He had one "not so normal" diaper that morning, but I did not think much of it. After the party, about half of the guests wound up sick. We thought food poisoning, but could not pinpoint the cause. In the end we think it was a stomach flu. The baby was fine after one diaper change, yet the adults were taken down for the count. How was I to know that would happen?

Germs are part of childhood, and hopefully you will avoid any major issues. Also, keep in mind that no matter how prepared you think you are, shit happens. Having a back-up plan with a neighbor or relative can provide peace of mind. I once was traveling home from a business trip, and was a few hours away from home. My husband had left earlier that morning for a flight out of town as well. I had my parents picking up my children from aftercare that day, knowing I would be home in the evening.

Sure enough, the call came from school that my daughter was sick. She had a fever and was doubled over in pain, and the school nurse was concerned it could be appendix or something more serious than the usual tummy troubles. I was hours away. Even if I ran to catch the next possible train home, I was still more than three hours from getting there. Luckily, I was able to get ahold of my parents and they were able to get to the school.

In the end, she had strep throat and after a few days of antibiotics she was fine. Self-doubt and mommy guilt always rears its ugly head in situations such as these. I had to remind myself that my daughter was fine, and that her grandma was taking good care of her. It is so easy to spiral into negativity when mommy guilt starts to take over our minds. Remember to put things into perspective. Having reliable back up plans can provide much needed confidence to handle whatever comes your way.

Potty Training: Enough Said

Potty training is such an individual thing. Every child is so different. I have heard, and know, many children who potty train after age three. It is not the end of the world. Frankly, diapers sometimes can be easier to deal with. The words, "Mommy I have to go potty," seem to happen at the absolute worst times.

I admit, I taught my three-year-old girl to squat in the mall parking lot once (maybe more than once) to avoid unbuckling the baby from the car seat and going all of the way back inside of the mall to find the nearest bathroom. I was smart enough to know we would not make it in time. Driving home quickly would at best have led to a urine soaked car seat, so I made my choice.

Thankfully it was summer and she was wearing plastic jelly shoes. I was worried someone would see me and judge my parenting. My negative self-talk was on high that day. What mom lets her three-year-old girl pee in the parking lot? Clearly, I was that mom. It is what it is. I am not particularly proud of it, but I have learned to let go of that particular guilt. One way to avoid that situation is to bring a little potty everywhere.

If you put a potty seat in the trunk of your car you can stop anywhere and use the potty in the back seat of the car. I would also suggest keeping toilet paper, big ziplock bags, and disinfectant spray as well.

Potty training is a huge source of stress for many families, and for others it just happens. My experience has taught me to start the conversation and let your toddler guide the process. I realize that is easier said than done, but I assure you, your child will get there. Each time we entered the potty training process I relied heavily on the day care center to help.

They did not believe in pull-ups at the school. It was diapers or big girl underwear, no in-between. The school's policy was based on the concept that pull-ups teach children to get used to feeling wet and can hamper progress. Ideally, this is supposed to make them learn they do not want to be wet, and they start to anticipate the pee pee. However, some kids just don't care if they are wet, and the pull-ups create a situation where they get used to feeling wet and then potty training becomes even tougher. True or not, we followed the guidance of the school.

My baby girl was a little over two-and-a-half-years-old, and I had just become pregnant with my son, so we decided it was time. We made a special trip to the store to pick out fancy princess-designed big girl underwear, and she was super excited to wear them. We spent the weekend without diapers, and she had accidents all weekend long. She helped me clean up each mess, and I did my best to show support and not frustration. No turning back.

The next day I sent her to the school with multiple changes of clothes and said, "Good Luck!"

I sent in all the pants and shorts she never wore. We were in a phase where she would ONLY wear skirts or dresses, and refused to put on pants. One accident that morning and she had to put on pants. That worked. No more accidents. I am convinced it was the fact that she had to change out of her pretty dress and put on pants that did it.

My son was not quite as easy. It was a longer process.

Sometimes, I learned, pull-ups are needed. Whether they contributed to the longer process I will never know, but we used them. It was especially important to use them at night. Despite taking longer, I learned to trust that he would learn to use the potty when he was ready.

Even when potty trained, bedwetting can be an issue. I know the parents of a lot of kids who kept the pull-ups or diapers for just sleeping for quite some time. Another option is to bring your child to the bathroom just before you, yourself, go to bed. Gently wake him or her up and take to the potty a few hours after bedtime. If accidents continue to happen at night beyond age six or seven, don't go into panic mode. Talk with your doctor; there are things that you can do to help. I assure you, are not alone.

> Potty training is a huge source of stress for many families, and for others it just happens. My experience has taught me to start the conversation and let your toddler guide the process.

Also, I found that it was important to put kids back in their own beds after an accident. I wondered if bringing my baby to bed with me because the bed was wet was reinforcing bedwetting, but changing all the sheets at three o'clock in the morning was a daunting task.

The trick I learned was to put hospital pads on the bed, above the mattress protector but under the sheet. This way, after an accident you can just pull off the one sheet and replace it. The mattress pad stays dry, and everyone can go back to their own beds again. They are inexpensive, and easy to find in the adult diaper section of most grocery stores.

Let's talk poop for a moment. This is a lot tougher. The phrase, "Mom, wipe my butt," seemed like it would be never-ending. I fantasized about the day I could go twenty-four hours without wiping anyone else's ass. That day did come, but not soon enough.

A lot of folks use food as a reward for potty training. I have mixed feeling about food as a reward, but I went with it. We used gummy fruit snacks because my son was obsessed with them, and M&M's are off-limits because of his sister's allergies. We would keep the fruit snacks in a tomato jar on the kitchen table. One morning, my toddler woke up before anyone else, and tried to sneak from the jar. He was about two-and-a-half, and we had just started potty training. Apparently, when the jar would not open he attempted to break it with a butcher knife.

> I fantasized about the day I could go twenty-four hours without wiping anyone else's ass. That day did come, but not soon enough.

When that did not work, he went back to bed. I woke up that Saturday morning to go into the kitchen and start breakfast to find a glass jar of gummy fruit snacks, a huge butcher knife, a steak knife, and the bathroom stool in the middle of my kitchen floor.

As my brain started to piece together how they got there, I was horrified at what could have happened. When I questioned him later that morning about it, he simply stated that he wanted fruit snacks. That was the day we put the baby gate back at the top of the stairs!

It may seem like it is never-ending, but I promise eventually the bathroom will be mastered, and the chances of you touching or smelling poo or pee will reduce considerably!

Hang in there—that day will come!

Daddy: Special Time

I will never forget that scan at the doctor's office when we learned our first was a girl. I was a tomboy as a child. My male cousin and I were born the same week and spent a lot of time together as small children. He was super athletic and into sports, cars and everything BOY. I wanted to be just like him. We were always competing. I wanted nothing to do with dolls, and what I considered the girly toys the family bought for me. I remember hours and hours at my grandmother's house playing with Matchbox cars and those awesome orange tracks.

According to my parents, I almost gave them a heart attack the day I reluctantly agreed to wear a dress to a grammar school concert. As the story goes, the spring concert was cancelled due to a snow day and my family never saw me in the dress, after all.

So when the time came for me to have my first child, I was torn between hoping for a boy or girl. After all, I was a girl, but I wasn't really sure I knew much about little girls.

My husband, on the other hand, was very sure he had absolutely no idea how to parent a little girl. He worked in a male dominated career, had very few, if any, female friends and no sisters. On the day of the sonogram where the doctor was able to tell us the sex of the baby, my husband was with me. The first thing he did after being told it was a girl was to ask our doctor on how certain she was of the sex. He literally asked the doctor to give him a percentage of certainty. After the doctor answered with, "Ninety-nine percent you are having a girl," he became quiet for the rest of the appointment. On the walk home through New York City, he continued to say nothing. I started to worry. Was he unhappy? What now? I knew he was scared, but I was frustrated that he was holding back from me.

Resist the urge to correct your spouse. He will not swaddle or feed or diaper the baby the way you do it, but if you don't let him do it, you will find yourself exhausted and frustrated.

Finally, I asked him to tell me what he was thinking and he said, "I like vanilla ice cream, but if someone handed me a chocolate cone, I would eat it." He was scared of the unknown and I knew that. He needed time to sort out in his mind how he felt. That was his way of processing. I knew at that moment he would be an amazing dad to his baby girl.

Fatherhood is defined in many ways by many people. To my husband, it is being a provider. It means making sure that his family has everything they need, even if that means he is always working. I have tried to set limits on how much he works, but I am often unsuccessful.

When the children were young, I asked that he come home by eight o'clock each night, so that he could spend time with our newborn while she was awake. It did not happen. I must admit, I did not mind as much as I let on, because it gave me more time with her after a long day of work myself.

My pediatrician at the time told me that until his children turned two years old, he was useless to his wife. I can't say it was any different at our house. He is a wonderful daddy and husband, but clearly parenting was not an instinct that kicks in right away for some men. Women, too. We always hear stories of how magical the moment is when you first lay eyes on your little angel. That makes for a great story, however I know lots of dads and moms who did not have the earth-shattering experience right off the bat. Having a baby is a new experience that can be magical and wonderful, but it can also be scary and uncomfortable. I remember those scary moments of fear and panic more than the happy bliss, myself. Don't beat yourself up, you are not alone. The happy moments just makes for a better story to tell.

I remember one of the first times I was on a business trip and my husband was on his own to get the baby dressed and off to day care. She was just under a year old and had woken up in the crib with diarrhea. It was everywhere. He could smell her room long before walking in. She was not crying or complaining, just full of poop. He stripped her down, and took her to the bathroom, and held her out like a turkey under the shower. Then he got her dressed and off to school with her bottles. The crib sheets and clothing he balled up and tossed in the bathtub for me to deal with when I got home that night. So many things are wrong with that situation, but in the end, baby was fine and got to school, I cleaned up the mess, and he and she survived the night without me.

When my son was born, my husband was better at helping out with the infant stage, although there were a few occasions when I was not at home that he waited for me to arrive to "notice" the diaper needed changing.

One funny story that hits home about male versus female priorities happened, as usual, when I was traveling. My husband had been home with both kids for a few days. My father stayed at our house to help my husband get the kids off to day care and help with dinner and bedtime so that my husband could go to work. I was running a training class a few hours drive away at the time, and my phone kept buzzing and buzzing. I stepped outside to answer, and my husband immediately began to tell me that the day care had called, the kids had rashes, and they need to be picked up.

First of all, what was I supposed to do about it while hours away? I asked him to go to the day care, get the kids, and take them to the pediatrician. He said he was home with a fever and couldn't get out of bed himself. Amazing how moms don't get sick days! Fine. I called my dad, and asked him to go check on the situation. Next thing I know my phone starts buzzing again. It is my husband. I answer, and I hear, "It's the boy and it's his penis I am on my way to the doctor now."

Huh: when "the kids" had a rash, no big deal. But the boy and the penis, that is urgent. I still make fun of him for that one. Turns out it was diaper rash. A little ointment and all better.

Clearly, my husband's instincts and mine are different. By constantly nagging him about how he was doing it wrong, I was creating more conflict than was needed. Resist the urge to correct your spouse. He will not swaddle, or feed, or diaper the baby the way you do it, but if you don't let him do it, you will find yourself exhausted and frustrated. Let him help even if it's not perfect. He will figure it out and the baby will be fine. They will bond with each other and you will rest. Let go of the idea that everything needs to be done the way you do it. You will only make yourself miserable. Let it be. Take the help in whatever form it comes.

What I learned while watching my husband with our children is to give him time to adjust, and he will be the wonderful daddy I always knew he could be. It just takes some guys a little longer to figure it out. If your spouse is like that, be patient, he will get there.

Birthdays: Stop the Madness

When I was a kid, I remember having a party at McDonald's. If I was lucky I got to have a few friends sleep over, too. There was no expensive entertainment, or fancy party destination. It was me and my friends playing board games, gossiping about boys, and having a Carvel ice cream cake. I remember a few basement parties where we played pin the tail on the donkey. We enjoyed every minute of it.

When did that become not good enough?

Kids' parties have gotten so elaborate and expensive. A big lesson for me, having spent a small fortune on some, and gone cheap on others, is that it doesn't really matter. Teaching kids that it isn't about the size and expense of a party, but about having fun with friends is well worth it in the long run.

When kids are little, parties are for parents. Let's face it, the first birthday party is the parents' way of saying that they survived the first year of parenthood, and now it is time to celebrate. I have been to first birthdays that rival wedding events. We did our first child's first birthday in the multipurpose room of our apartment building. Not too extravagant, but a lot of fun.

The first birthday can be a good way to get to know

other families by inviting kids from your day care, or it can be a reason to bring your extended family together. Just remember it is more about your memories than your baby's. Whether you have a houseful of people or just take a photo of your baby having his or her first birthday cake, the baby doesn't know the difference!

We have attended a few over the top parties over the years, and if that is something that is important to you and in your budget, I say go for it! If it is not in the budget, do not feel you need to do it just because the other families are. It's okay to stop the madness, and don't feed into any mommy guilt here!

One particular party we attended was in New York City at a place with arts and crafts, food, and then a petting zoo. Literally, a petting zoo in a New York City Midtown building! The toddlers were able to play with live lambs and bunnies and reptiles. Who knew you could do that? I had to ask the parents the cost—no matter how rude I must have seemed. If I remember correctly it was approximately $1,000 to have a dozen or so kids. Wow! It can be easy to fall into the trap of feeling like you need to make "the best party ever." Especially today watching parents posting parties on Facebook and Pinterest. It may seem like everyone else has their shit together more than you, and that they are creating amazing memories and perfect parties, but the reality is the kids don't care that much about what you spend. They just want to have fun. Fun does not need to be elaborate or over the top.

Alcohol or not? That is such a personal choice. Frankly I sometimes appreciate getting to have a glass of wine as I hang around with other parents watching a bunch of toddlers running around like maniacs. At a backyard party with the family it may be fun to have grown-up food and drinks, but a princess tea party or bouncy house—not so much. In the end, the party is about the child, not about us. Keep in mind when you have a toddler the parents tend to stay, so plan to have lots of moms and dads around. I have learned that morning parties were easy for me in the younger years because I could get bagels, coffee and OJ for the kids, and then just have cake. It is cheaper and everyone was happy.

As the kids get older it becomes "drop-off parties." It can be cheaper as far as food goes, however make sure you have enough grown-ups there to help. A bunch of grade school kids can be overwhelming alone. If your budget is tight, have the party in the afternoon before dinner but after lunch. Put "cake only" on the invitation so that the kids will have had lunch.

Don't let yourself get upset if you can not pull off the perfect Pinterest cake or craft. Your kids will still love it if they are involved in planning it and executing it. The important part is having fun and celebrating with friends.

No one really needs pizza in the middle of the afternoon. They just want the cake after all. This will save on cost, especially if you do the party out of your home. Indoor playgrounds, bouncy house places, the YMCA, rock climbing, roller-skating, and pottery studios are all birthday parties we have done with some success.

Another good idea I've seen some parents do successfully is the fake sleepover. Kids come in PJs with stuffed animals in hand and watch a movie and popcorn, order pizza and do a craft and cake. Parents can pick up around ten o'clock in the evening. No kids stay overnight, but they feel as if it was something special because it is late at night.

We had the "fake sleepover" one year and instead of cake we made our own version of those yogurt shops that seem so popular now. We had vanilla ice cream and I put out bowls with lots of unique toppings so the kids could create their own special desserts. We had candy, cereal, crackers, pretzels, and any other treat we could find. The dessert also became an activity. It was messy, but super fun!

The best and most economical party idea we have done is the nail salon. It worked at age four, and again at ten. If you have a local nail salon within walking distance (strip malls work well) to a pizza place, have the girls dropped off at salon and get manicures and then walk over to have pizza. You just need to bring cake. Easy, inexpensive, and the kids loved it at both ages.

When it comes to gifts, be prepared to get duplicates and a lot of re-gifted junk. The loud annoying toys most likely are re-gift, but you can put them away and re-gift them yourself at some point. My suggestion is to only re-gift duplicate gifts you can't return. If you get a really bad gift with a broken box and it is something no kid would want, do not re-gift it. Break the pattern. Another idea is to pick up toys on sale when you see them and keep a stock pile of presents. When parties come up, you can have your child "shop" in the party closet to find the perfect gift for the party. This can also save you from making the last minute stop to the drug store for a gift certificate on the way to a party you are already late for. Can you tell I have made that trip more than once?

We attended a birthday party for a young boy around Christmas whose mom requested we donate to St. Jude Hospital in lieu of a gift. What a great idea when kids are so small they do not really know the difference! I brought it up as an option with my kids a few times, but did not push the issue. My daughter did it twice. I was so proud of her choice. She was five or six, and I let her choose the charity and send a letter requesting her friends take whatever they would have spent on a gift and write a check to that particular charity. After her party she sent the letter with all the checks to the organization. Having her learn how good it feels to do acts of kindness is such a wonderful lesson. That being said, they are kids, and if they choose not to do it, do not read into it. Kids want gifts, after all birthdays are only once a year. My son never agreed to it and my daughter has chosen to go with her own gifts the following years.

You do not need to go crazy to have a birthday party. There are so many great ideas if you search the internet. Just don't let yourself get upset if you can not pull off the perfect Pinterest cake or craft. Your kids will still love it if they are involved in planning it and executing it. The important part is having fun and celebrating with friends.

Get Organized: Sort Of

Did you have visions of motherhood that looked neat and organized like a Norman Rockwell painting? Yep, I did. But that was so not my reality.

Being organized is something I quickly learned was a necessity for me as a mom and not just for the obvious reasons. For me it was crucial to have some level of control to keep my sanity. Never finding crap at the bottom of my purse was one thing, but not having a binky the moment my little girl started to have a meltdown: that was completely another.

My diaper bag was the first place I found I needed to master. Many diaper bags are wonderful, with a gazillion pockets and ways to get organized, yet I found that I never quite found the one that satisfied my need for a particular level of organization.

That is when I created my own system. I found a big carry-all bag with a zipper, so when bending over to pick up a toy, bottle, binky or crying toddler I did not spill the entire contents of the bag all over the floor. The key, I found, was investing in different size cosmetic bags, preferably mesh and in bright solid colors. I had one for the sippy or bottle along with the powdered formula. One for the little toys. One to hold diapers and wipes. One for snacks. One for emergency epinephrine meds. One for the inhaler. One for pens and sticky notes. One for binkies. One for soft books. One for my stuff, such as chapstick, telephone, aspirin, etc.

You get the picture. I created my own system, color-coded and all. It was the best. If I needed to change bags or take more or less items one day, I was able to adjust quickly. That simple step was a sanity saver, for sure. I am long out of the diaper phase, yet I continue to use the same system.

It's not just about diaper bags. Having kids creates chaos and mess. If you have an overwhelming need to keep your ducks in a row, it can make all the difference to find little tricks to keep you sane.

I must admit my favorite stores are ones that sell baskets and folders and containers. I am always striving for that ideal level of order, despite the fact that I know it will never be as good as I imagine it. Letting go of control issues can be challenging. Especially since having a baby means that so many things we had control over have gone right out the window.

Do the best you can, and remember to give yourself a break. You, your kids, and your house will be more disorganized than you like. Let it go. Do not let guilt take over. If you have a playdate at your house and your kitchen sink is full of dirty dishes, so what! Who cares? If the playdate parent judges you for it, so be it. More than likely she will be relieved to see she is not the only one. I once read somewhere that between a clean house, happy kids, and mom's sanity we can only pick two. One always has to give. I have to agree. If I think about it, two of those three can happen at once, but all three at the same time is nearly impossible.

Kids equal mess. Mess equals kids. The faster you

accept it, the happier mommy you will be. That being true, I have learned a few tricks and ways to keep organized and minimize the chaos.

First, as I mentioned earlier, is definitely the diaper bag. That took some trial and error, but was well worth it. That need does not end when potty training is complete. The system of pockets or mini pouches comes in handy as the kids grow as well. You would be surprised at the quantity of stuff you still need to carry. Never underestimate the power of a well-organized bag!

Another tip I found is for the toys. So many toys everywhere! Amazing how a tiny baby can have so much stuff! Especially when the kids are little, there is a big need for a way to organize it all. I learned that it is not necessary to spend a fortune on expensive organizing systems and baskets and shelves.

Go to the dollar store or cheap home goods stores and pick up pretty baskets in all sizes.

Never finding crap at the bottom of my purse was one thing, but not having a binky the moment my little girl started to have a meltdown, that was completely another.

Keep many of the toys in a closet, or if you're lucky, a basement area. Take a bunch of the stuff that you want to have in the common areas of the house and put them in the baskets. When the kids get tired of the toys, rotate the stuff in the closet. Every week, switch out the toys so the kids get variety and are not bored, but you do not need to see everything clogging up your space every day. Your family room does not need to look like a preschool at all times.

The same concept is true of sippy cups and other bright colored things in the kitchen. We have kitchen cabinets with glass doors, which makes it tough to hide those ugly bottles and cups. I found inexpensive baskets to put in my kitchen cabinets to keep the plastic ones from being seen from every angle of my kitchen.

Another area that created chaos in my organized mind was the barrage of school papers that came home daily. An unbelievable amount of paper and "mommy homework" seems to get sent home from school, starting from day one. When I would go on business trips I would come home to piles of papers on my kitchen or dining room table and it would drive me "bat-shit crazy." The mail, the school papers, the drawings, the notes, and the important stuff together in a big messy pile. I would feel the need to clean it up before I could even sit down and relax. As expected, I was delinquent on more than a few important school papers and deadlines.

> I believe in giving age appropriate responsibilities early on. Kids can vacuum and load and empty the dishwasher and do other small chores themselves.

I know those beautiful pictures and school work mean a lot, but you really don't need to keep it all. I have a hallway and a basement with framed kid art I swap out periodically, but for the most part I feel okay tossing a lot of it.

I created a couple of places and systems that work for me. First, the mail. I have a big basket on my desk that acts as an "in-box." Anyone who takes in the mail knows it goes in mommy's in-box. I can then go through it and make sure that it goes to the right place. I pay bills or put items on my husband's desk or toss or put it away. No more piles around the house, everything in the basket.

Next, the school stuff. It goes in the kitchen under the

dry erase magnet board with the calendars, invites, coupons, and to do lists in two mounted file folders. I have tried different types and currently I like wire baskets. They are useful and still look pretty. Each one is labeled. The kids come in from school, empty their backpacks themselves, and put all papers from school folders into the file baskets hanging on the wall. They are responsible for emptying lunch boxes and folders and putting their backpacks away. The lunch thing is tough for my son. I have found bananas mushed into pockets days later—not pretty! Just last week I pulled a ziplock bag with a funny colored liquid that I believe was cut up red peppers at one point. Thankfully, that bag held up without breaking open! Like everything, it is a work in progress.

One mistake a lot of us make is to do it for the kids because we want it done right. I believe in giving age appropriate responsibilities early on. A kindergartener is fully able to empty his or her backpack on a daily basis. Kids can vacuum, load and empty the dishwasher, and do other small chores themselves. By having my kids empty school folders on their own, I don't deal with messy papers throughout my kitchen. I can go through the folder later when kids are in bed. If there is something I need to read or sign I can do it at that point, and then put it right into the backpacks for the next day. The rest of the stuff gets kept or tossed.

Each of my kids has a big plastic file box kept in a closet. There are thirteen files in each one labeled K-12. I keep about an inch worth of papers for each school year and file them in the box. When they get older and want to look through their old papers, they can go to the file box. I only save select papers that they may get a kick out of seeing later in life. Recycle and toss the rest. It is okay.

Your kids will be fine if you do not cherish every single time they put pencil to paper.

Clothes can also be a source of mess and chaos. The older kids get, the more chores they are capable of doing. Putting clothes away can be tricky, especially hanging. Two tips I learned are to either add another rod in the closet to hang clothes where the kids can reach them, or use shoe and sweater organizers. The sweater bins are great for organizing clothes. I have also found that for younger kids, the shoe organizers work well. You can fit two to four items in each compartment and then you can organize the closet by type of shirt, as well as color code items that go together. You can even label them to make it easier for little ones to put stuff away themselves. It may not be as neat as you would like it to be, but it will help them be more independent, and save you some time. Another closet tip is to create space where one does not exist. A mud room to dump stuff is a wonderful luxury, one I do not have. Instead, my side door has a bench and hooks and a place for shoes, but not much else. What I do have is a full bathroom right by the side door in the family room where no one showers, so it was wasted space.

> Do the best you can and remember to give yourself a break. You, your kids, and your house will be more disorganized than you like. Let it go.

I created what we call the crapper closet. I put a rod in the shower for coats and added a sweater holder to the rod. I put scarves, pool towels and beach bags, baseball gloves, tennis rackets, soccer stuff, field hockey sticks, etc. All the stuff you want by the door that becomes a problem when you have no space for it.

Be creative, think outside the box, or shower, and you

can surprise yourself with the ideas you can come up with. Keep in mind, having kids does not means disorganized chaos has to be the norm, however accept imperfection and lose the guilt. Keep the happy kids, and your sanity, and don't sweat the rest.

Back to School: Yay!

I must admit, I did not volunteer or become active in my children's school for a long time. Parent meetings were during the day, and I was working. I used to get to Back to School night early to be the first to sign up for the eight o'clock parent-teacher conference slot, so that I could go before work hours. Otherwise, it meant taking a half a day off. I often was struck by mommy guilt over not being involved. In the last year I have taken opportunities to take on more roles in the Parent Teacher Organization and volunteer in the classroom.

Whether I was present in the school or not seemed to have very little impact on how much my children liked or embraced school. I found it was more important to show interest in what kids do at school and keep an open dialogue than actually being there all the time. My advice would be to do what you can, but don't beat yourself up over what you can not do. Asking questions and showing interest motivates kids for learning.

My daughter loves school and puts lots of pressure on herself. I need to remind her that there is more to school than just her grades. I want her to enjoy learning and focus on what she likes and is good at. She constantly wants me to check her homework and see what she is doing in school. She is self-motivated.

My son seems to like school, but when I try to work with him on his homework he says, "Mom, I don't care if it isn't spelled right, that's the teacher's job." Two different kids, two different approaches. I try to support their strengths and not get too hung up on the rest.

> As parents we may find ourselves not spending time focusing on where our children excel and thrive. Being aware that what we focus on becomes their inner dialogue later in life is a good reminder to nurture and celebrate strengths.

When report cards arrive, we, as parents, often focus on the lowest grades. We look for areas of improvement needed and explore deficiencies rather than celebrating accomplish-ments. This creates inner dialogue for our kids that they carry with them throughout their lives. So many of us have self-critical internal dialogue and struggle with perfec-tionism. It starts with messages we get as children.

Being aware that what we focus on becomes their inner dialogue later in life is a good reminder to nurture and celebrate strengths.

I catch myself repeating this negative pattern with my children. I scan the report card and the teachers' notes to see what they need to do better. I compare them to the other kids in the class and ask questions such as, "So tell me why the teacher says you need support with prewriting skills. What's going on?" I have learned to stop myself from scanning for the lowest grade, and instead focus on the most positive areas. Praise them for the effort they put into their school work versus the actual grades themselves. I see how my perfectionism has not served me well, and now I work to consciously break the pattern with my kids. As parents, we want success for our children. I have learned that for my family, success is less about people-pleasing, perfectionism, and getting all A's, and more about healthy striving, resiliency, and learning.

Having two children with different views on school, I focus on what each of them like about it. Asking how school was today is usually met with "fine." I try to ask about what they are learning, what they did that was fun, or with whom they sat at lunch. I am interested in who they are becoming, who they choose to be friends with, and why and what they like and don't like, just as much as in perfomance.

Homework can be such a source of stress, for not only kids, but parents as well. Homework can create conflict and frustration, or it can improve confidence and competencies. How much should parents help and how much should we let them figure it themselves? I am more hands-off with homework. I remember walking the halls of the grammar school looking at projects on bulletin boards. There were clear differences between the kids whose parents helped and those who did it themselves. Sometimes I would feel guilty that I did not spend more time helping with projects, however that quickly subsided when I reminded myself of the benefits of accomplishing something on their own.

When my daughter was in second grade, she won a bookmark contest. She was asked to draw an animal. She asked me to draw the outline for her to color in. Instead, I encouraged her to do the best she could on her own. She made a cute little monkey that was clearly all her own. She was so proud when she won the contest and the entire school was given a copy of her bookmark monkey!

Sports: Organized Sports or Backyard Play?

What can you say when your child tells you that you don't support her dreams of going to the Olympics? Ugh... really?

She tells you Gabby Douglas's parents sent her across the country to be good enough to train for the Olympics, and all I am asking for is blah blah blah.

It is great for kids to be involved in sports early on, but understand that not all kids find what they like right away. Try different things and encourage an active lifestyle by modeling behavior through going to the gym or playing on an adult team of some sort.

I hear from many parents that in order to have success, kids must pick a sport and start playing competitively as early as possible. It is easy to fall into that pattern. I don't agree it is the only way to go. Parents often dream of tuition-free college via sports, and want to create their unrealized dreams through their children. It can be tough to resist.

We experience that scenario often in our home. My son likes sports: any sport, all sports. He does well and gets opportunities to play on competitive teams, and my husband could not be happier. I often see my husband's love of baseball motivate him to push our son harder at it than with any other sport. My husband was a college football player who I am sure now thinks, "what if," and sees a chance for his boy to go further with baseball, football, or soccer.

What happens when kids are totally focused on one sport and then decide they don't want to do it any longer? Do you force them to keep going? Do you let them do something different?

We often put so much pressure on kids to be good at sports that it makes me wonder if that is really the best way to go. I hope to encourage variety and let kids learn what they like by trial and effort.

> When it comes to sports and extra-curricular activities, I hope to encourage variety and let my kids learn what they like by trial and effort.

My son keeps talking about how he is going to be a pro football player some day, and watches and plays any sport he can. I want to encourage a love of being active without pushing him to the point it is no longer fun. My daughter wanted to be an Olympic gymnast last year, but she also likes to play field hockey and softball. Now she does not even do gymnastics. I enjoy seeing them have fun and build confidence as well as learn to lose gracefully. When it is no longer fun it is time to do something else.

The more sports kids try, the more they build up different skills. Eventually they will figure out what they want to spend more time doing. My advice is try not to stress too early if they don't show much interest in sports. Don't feel as if you have missed a window of opportunity.

The reality is, your kid is most likely not going to wind up a professional sports stars. That's okay. Sorry to burst your bubble. They will learn how to win and lose gracefully, be a part of a team, and gain a sense of accomplishment and pride. Provide opportunities to have fun and figure out what they like to do, and hopefully they will take a love of sports into adulthood as a part of a confident, active and healthy lifestyle.

Your Health: Diet & Exercise, Maybe

Eat healthy and exercise…you know it is important, and yet you still finish off the kid's macaroni and cheese or eat the crust you take off of sandwiches. If you are like most moms I know, sometimes things are going well and sometimes you just need to sit and eat an entire sleeve of thin mints. Stop beating yourself up about it.

I see all the pictures of the in-shape moms with perfect flat stomach who are back to pre-pregnancy shape in no time. It happens to some women—definitely—but not most of us. Our bodies change.

That saying, "I wish I weighed the same as when I first thought I was fat." Does that ring a bell?

I was told by my OB/GYN that if I gained too much I would end up about ten pounds bigger after each baby. No way, I thought. I was going to prove her wrong.

Nope. I gained sixty with each baby and after lots of ups and downs and ups and downs, and two kids, I pretty much leveled out twenty pounds bigger than when I found out I was pregnant for the first time.

It would be so great to be twenty (or thirty) pounds lighter, however having a daughter, I am very aware of how much she is bombarded with unhealthy images of women and women's bodies. I don't talk fat or diet (or at least I make a very strong effort not to) around her. We talk about health and about balance. I try to show her I am comfortable in my own skin. I try to love my big booty and curves. I joke with my husband that I married a big guy so I could appear petite. That being said, my body is strong and healthy and I don't worry about finishing the crust of pizza or having an Oreo or two with my husband after the kids go to bed. Not every day, but everything in moderation. After all, to my kids I am the most beautiful woman in the world!

> I see all the pictures of the in-shape moms with perfect flat stomach who are back to pre-pregnancy shape in no time. It happens to some women—definitely — but not most of us. Our bodies change.

I go to the gym and exercise—spin class and cardio and weights. Some weeks four or five times, and other weeks once. It is what it is. I personally do not enjoy working out. I know some people do. They get that "runners high." I have no concept of that. I just know that it is something I need to do, and I feel better after I am done.

I have gone to the YMCA, joined very expensive gyms, and worked out with CDs and the elliptical in the basement. All of them work if you do them. As long as I get up and do something a few times a week I am happy. I have learned that expensive gyms are usually not much better than less expensive options. I have tried them all at different points, and don't see a huge difference.

Working out at home sometimes can work too. It is a great way for the kids to get involved with exercise and to model the right behaviors. When I do a workout video in the basement early in the morning, the kids will come downstairs and try to do what I do. It can make it more challenging, but makes for wonderful bonding and learning.

Diets can be a minefield of contradicting information. You could go vegan, or paleo, or count calories, or a host of other options. Best bet is to speak to a nutritionist if you want to eliminate one food or another. Teaching you how to choose fruit over candy, or salad over junk food the majority of the time will go a long way if started early.

The bottom line is, it is important to eat healthy. Have lots of veggies and greens and limit the red meat and the cheese and sugar. I keep the weekdays as healthy as reasonably possible and enjoy the weekend chips, and guacamole, and burgers, and beer or wine. I believe in everything in moderation. That is what works for me. You will also find what works for you knowing that how you choose to eat will have an impact on what your kids choose.

The most important thing I have learned is that it is important to feel strong and healthy and happy. That means that you should try to do the best that you can and love yourself, and show your kids a healthy relationship with food and with exercise as well as to have a love and appreciation for your body with all its curves and soft parts.

Food Allergies: No Nuts, Please

I could probably write an entire book on this topic, and yet many of you who are reading this are not directly affected by it, so I will try to limit the lecturing.

Food allergies are something my family deals with daily. If you are blessed to not have a child with food allergies, chances are kids in school or friends do have allergies. Being sensitive to your children's friends' needs will help them to remain friends.

The first thing I learned as a mom with a child with food allergies is that often, the people you count on to keep your kids safe—parents, teachers, school administrators, etc., think you are crazy. The idea that something basic and simple that most children eat, carry, touch, have smeared on their clothing etc., could kill your child—that can make you crazy! It is a tough concept to fully understand. I even know parents of kids with allergies who don't always get it. Unfortunately, kids with allergies who find themselves without emergency epinephrine, can have made a deadly mistake.

Food allergies have, and still do, bring out intense feelings of guilt and helplessness. Could I have done something different? After all, I ate peanut butter often when pregnant with my daughter. Peanut butter and jelly on white bread was a favorite. When I became pregnant with my second child I asked the allergist about it, and the answer at that moment was, "We don't really know what causes it but stay away from nuts with this pregnancy." Well of course I was going to stay away from nuts, we were a nut-free house! I felt awful. I was convinced it was my fault.

From what I have read, the medical community is still searching for definitive answers on causality. Just recently I read that peanut allergy may be caused by nut particles in the dust and air that penetrate the skin of children with eczema. The breaks in the skin from eczema and scratching as well as lotions and creams contribute to the faulty immune response to nuts. The more research I do, the more confusing it is. Rationally, I understand I did not intentionally cause or wish this allergy on my child, however that does not ease the pain and sadness I feel every time she is excluded from an activity, or goes into a mini panic attack if someone near her has a bag of nuts or PB&J sandwich. My heart breaks for her when I think about the burden she carries every day just to stay safe.

Just yesterday we went to a restaurant we had never been before. I called ahead and asked about the menu to be sure that they did not use peanut oil or have excessive nuts on the menu. Finding completely nut-free restaurants are rare, and I believe it is important to learn how to be safe when eating out. When we arrived at the restaurant we asked the waiter about nuts on the menu and he stated that they fry in peanut oil. Immediately my daughter began to cry and express frustration. We informed the waiter that the person who we spoke to said they use soybean. He then went back into the kitchen and spoke to the chef. It turns out they had switched from peanut oil a year or so before and the waiter was not told. We made the decision to stay and have dinner, however it was excruciating to watch my daughter agonize over the menu to make a decision she felt comfortable eating. It is never easy.

When she was first diagnosed with allergies I admit I did not get it. It can be such a strange concept. I read once that having allergens such as peanuts in the classroom is like sending your child to school with a poisonous snake roaming the classroom. You have very little ability to know when and if it will strike. That created an image that stuck with me. No one would realistically be comfortable sending their child into that environment, but allergy parents are expected to trust that their kids are safe when they go to school, even in the presence of deadly allergens. When parents insist their child's rights are harmed because they don't eat anything else but peanut butter, it can be absolutely infuriating. Your child will not starve to death, and eventually he or she will eat what you give him or her to eat. Alternatives like sunflower or soy are pretty good, too. On white bread with some jelly it's really tough to tell the difference.

As a baby, my firstborn was easy going and pleasant just about all the time. Not cranky or fussy. I was blessed. I nursed for about a month and then moved to formula. Two weeks into formula feeding she cried and cried. It was twenty-four hours of cranky hell. It felt as if my sweet baby had been taken over by a demon. Nothing consoled her. I called the pediatrician and he said to put her on non-dairy formula. That was the beginning of food becoming the center of our universe.

Once I switched her formula it was as if a light switched on. She was fine again. As she grew older we avoided dairy. At about five to six months old, I took her to pediatrician because she always had boogers. She had non-stop congestion. We could not tell if it was the "daycare cold" or if it was something else. We were sent to the allergist who skin tested her and she came up positive for dairy and egg. We became somewhat dairy-free, replacing it with soy everything. I must admit the frozen organic soy mac-n-cheese was pretty good, but soy yogurt—not so much. We thought we had it under control.

When she was about nine months old, I gave her one plain piece of chocolate—she vomited. I thought—huh—dairy, I guess. It was a candy that said, "May contain peanut," and I did not realize what the real problem was until years later.

> If you are blessed to not have a child with food allergies, chances are kids in school or friends will have allergies. Being sensitive to your children's friends' needs will help them to remain friends.

At eighteen months old we went on a family vacation to Aruba. We were eating dinner in an Argentinian steak house, and I gave her a small bite of my steak. She broke out in head to toe hives and was crying and scratching. We were so scared. I did not understand the risk of anaphylaxis, and had no Benadryl or emergency medication.

We went back to the hotel and waited it out. Looking back, I realize how dangerous that could have been—we had no idea. At one point I walked to the bathroom and locked the door in panic. I knew in my heart that my husband was calm and had her comforted. I just needed to not be in the room. I was overwhelmed with fear. Not my proudest moment. Instead, it is a moment that still brings tinges of guilt and regret knowing what could have occurred. After some time, the hives subsided and she was fine. As soon as the trip was over we went to the allergist to find out what happened that day. We had no idea.

We saw the allergist and she again had allergy tests. Dairy and egg were all fine. She had outgrown her allergies to them. So what the heck caused the hives? The doctor told us maybe it was nothing. I kind of thought that was a crappy answer, so I switched doctors. I had told him she had gotten some random hives on her wrist but nothing as bad as in Aruba, and he said maybe it was emotional. I got hives as a small child. I had been told as a child I was allergic to cat hair. My mother also told me that I was an emotional child and would break out in hives when I was upset or crying. I am not really sure what the cause was, maybe it was an emotional reaction, or maybe it was a food reaction, or contact allergy and I became emotional because I was having a reaction. Seems to me emotions and hives are linked, however casually, a bit like the chicken and egg. I have noticed with my daughter that emotions tend to exacerbate reactions when hives appear.

I have also learned that it is important to get a second opinion.

I have said it before: Be sure to trust your instincts. When the doctor brushed off the event in Aruba I knew it was time to get another opinion. Remember that doctors are only human, and you know your child better than anyone else does. When healthcare providers can't find a diagnosis or cause for symptoms, parents often start to create worst-case scenarios in their heads. This leads to stress, guilt, and fear. Understand that you are your child's best advocate. Don't feed into the self-blame; focus your energy on finding an answer and trust your instincts.

I was able to find an allergist in New York City and had my daughter tested for multiple allergens. The test gave us the news that she was allergic to peanut and most tree nuts. We still had no idea why she would randomly get hives, so I was asked to keep a food diary for months and months, and tested several foods based on what we learned. Eventually the doctor tested her for garlic. Sure enough, that was it. She reacted to hummus, tomato sauce, crackers, miso soup. Garlic gave her hives. Italian kid from Jersey and allergic to garlic!

In the process of testing and finding the culprit for the hives, we learned her blood levels for nuts and specifically peanuts, were extremely high. That is when we were given our first EpiPen® and learned what anaphylaxis is and how to handle it. We did not get it at first. My husband and I would eat nuts when she was asleep or not in the room, however over time we learned that was risky. We also learned that everyone has a different level of risk tolerance, and it is important to respect that comfort levels vary.

We find it tough enough when people do the eye roll or seem to be annoyed when my daughter says she is not comfortable eating something because of a risk of nut cross-contamination. It can be really hard for others to understand the risk involved with foods that come into contact with allergens. For example, bread made on shared equipment with almonds or walnuts could lead to a reaction for my daughter. Reactions are not predictable. It could be vomit, hives, or anaphylaxis. There is no way to predict. People who do not live with this every day do not always understand the risks, and as a child it can be very hard to communicate to adults or to friends when they don't feel safe. It is annoying. So, for those other parents who are annoyed by the allergy, I get it. I am annoyed. My daughter is annoyed, too.

It would be awesome to sit down to a meal and not

read every label, or not ask twenty questions of the waiter or cook or host. Unfortunately, that is not an option for us. Asking the question, "Does this contain nuts" is not enough.

As a mom I have taught my daughter, from a young age, to say, "No, thank you" to anything homemade or without a label to read. She also has memorized which brands label things well and which don't. Manufacturers are only required to label if the item contains allergens. The "may contain" statements or "made on equipment with" label is voluntary, and not mandated. Knowing which companies are better than others is important. It does not feel good when others appear annoyed, but I have learned not to let what others think bother me when it comes to staying safe. I instill in my daughter to just be polite and respectful, and understand that you can't control the way others respond. You also will never starve to death by going all day or all afternoon without eating, and there will always be safe food when you get home.

Practicing using the expired injection needles on fruit can also be a great way to help empower kids with allergies to take charge of their safety and feel confident they can handle any situation.

After having food challenges and blood tests, the bottom line for us is to keep a nut-free home. We learned to read all labels and how to be safe. A lesson I learned is to try to not make my daughter anxious about it. I am not saying I was successful, she definitely gets anxious and she would rather not eat than take chances, however, the older she gets, both she and I are getting better about being safe without unnecessary anxiety. Kids with food allergies often have anxiety and stress, especially in social situations. As parents, we can help reduce their anxiety when we reduce our own. It is so important for us to manage our anxiety and fear by taking care of our mental health. It is important to understand the big picture, know how to stay safe, and have a plan for dealing with an allergic reaction.

For us, we know how to use our epinephrine pen (commonly known as an EpiPen®). We have the one that talks you through it, which gives us an extra sense of security in an emergency. We follow the doctor's plan, check in with him yearly, and carry all medications and copies of the emergency plan at all times.

Not only is it important to know what to do in an emergency, but also identify what an emergency looks like. When do you give antihistamines, steroid or injections? What symptoms mean that you should go right to injection, as opposed to symptoms that just need an antihistamine? At the risk of giving medical advice without a license, I would say you want to be sure to go over your emergency plan with your physician carefully. If you are caring for another child with allergies, you want to ask questions about the emergency plan.

The more kids know what to do, the more confident they will become. Knowledge is power. My daughter started to carry her own medicine by about ten years old, and she has a copy of her emergency plan with her at all times. Practicing how to give herself an injection by using the expired needles on fruit can also be a great way to help empower kids with allergies to take charge of their safety and feel confident they can handle any situation.

As I said before, attitude can make all the difference. Some kids are able to look at the upside to their allergies by recognizing that they are more accountable for the food they put in their bodies. They read all labels and become educated on not only how to stay safe, but how to eat healthier and have an understanding of what is in the things that they eat.

One Easter we attended an Easter egg hunt in town. I don't know why I assumed it would be nut free, but I was wrong. When I learned the eggs on the church lawn had peanut butter and all kinds of candy, I discussed it with my kids. They were told that they could both hang with friends and participate in the hunt, but that my daughter could not pick up, touch, or eat any candy or eggs. My son could search for eggs, collect them, but only eat candy without nuts or peanut butter. Nothing was to come back into the house. He was asked to give any nut candy to other kids.

My daughter was fine with it. She was happy to be a part of the hunt. My son, not so much. He was crying and wanted to go home. I had to do quite a lot of convincing to get him to stay and agree to the rules despite the fact that he was able to do so much more than she was. It really comes down to perspective and attitude. My daughter saw the situation as a chance to hang out with her friends and enjoy being on the hunt for candy. My son only focused on the fact that he could not eat ALL of the candy.

Overall, when it comes to food allergies I learned that others don't always understand, and that the best thing to do is to know your emergency plan, understand the level of risk you are comfortable with, be consistent with staying safe, and most importantly do not panic. Have medicine with you at all times. Too often, stories of tragedy involve eating something with unknown allergens and not getting to emergency medicine quickly enough. This is true for parents and kids, siblings and friends as well.

Understand that pleasing other people is not as

important as being safe. Strangely, some people become offended if they tell me something is nut-free and we choose not to eat it anyway. But I try to not let it bother me anymore if they are offended. Unless you are absolutely sure of all ingredients and the conditions of how it was made, it's not worth taking chances. An annoyed friend is not really a friend when it comes to safety. I have also learned not to make a huge deal of it, especially in public.

For example, for a person with severe allergies, just asking a restaurant manager which ingredients are used in certain meals may not be enough. You may want to know how closely the ingredient your child is allergic to is kept to other ingredients in the kitchen, or how often kitchen staff change gloves. Some managers may be offended, or feel that you are just being nosy or overbearing by asking these questions. Be polite, then make an educated decision whether to eat in that restaurant based on the answers. Don't try to lecture or educate the manager. The middle of the dinner hour is not the time or place. And if the person you are questioning perceives you as a pest, he or she may just tell you what they think you want to hear.

An annoyed waiter saying, "Yes, yes, no nuts," is not reassuring, and you could wind up in more risk. Do homework before going somewhere, and limit what questions need to be asked in the actual restaurant. There are plenty of ways to get detailed information online or by calling ahead. Planning ahead gives you greater comfort at the restaurant.

For parents who are blessed to not have children with food allergies I would say please understand that kids with allergies did not ask for them, and they certainly are not exaggerating the risk. They are not looking to ruin your party or event, they just want to be safe like everyone else.

Imagine your child being handed an ice-cream cone with rat poison or a deadly chemical sprinkled on top and being told to just "brush it off" before eating the ice cream. Of course you would not let your child continue to eat the ice cream, yet that situation is the reality for many for kids with life threatening allergies.

One last piece of advice for those parents who have kids with allergies: Go easy on yourself. It is so easy to become overwhelmed and anxious about staying safe. You can only control so much. I have found that websites and groups for parents of kids with allergies are super helpful for learning about new studies, recalls, resources, and new nut free foods. On the flip side, being part of those communities can also increase anxiety. If you spend too much time on those sites or in those groups, you will find yourself taking in not only resources, but reading the tragedies and horror stories of children who had reactions, including some who died as a result.

When I find myself reading articles while crying uncontrollably, I know it is time to take a step back. Anxiety can become overwhelming and paralyzing when it grows. The more you spend time reading about it, the harder it will be to focus your energy on staying safe. Anxiety serves a purpose: To make us aware of danger. But spending too much time looking at what can go wrong is also a problem. It is easy to let it get out of control. Keep an eye on it. Try to find a balance between getting education and support without being consumed. Remember to take a step back and put it into perspective.

Your child is not his or her food allergies. She or he is a wonderful, beautiful, kind and spectacular kid who happens to have food allergies. Just because it is a part of everyday life does not mean it needs to be your entire life.

Lice: Oh Crap, Not Again

I must admit I have learned more than I want to know about this topic. My head becomes itchy just thinking about it.

My first fall living in the suburbs I heard about head lice in the schools. My oldest was in preschool and I thought, "No way, that's for dirty kids, how could we possibly get head lice?"

Don't get me wrong, my kids are often dirty and I admit it is really easy to skip bath time. But no way could we have "buggies." Well, I could not have been more wrong—about everything. With a newborn baby, a three-year-old, a new home, a hectic work schedule, my three-year-old got "the buggies."

I had heard tea tree oil can help, so I put a crapload in my hair and in her hair and panicked. I went to the pediatrician and the tea tree oil made the bugs more active than usual, so all I did was go within a foot of the doctor and she said, "Wow yes, I have never seen it like that."

This was not going to be good. We were infested.

My first thought after "oh shit" was the family we were with the night before. We had had dinner at someone else's house and she was pregnant. The last thing I wanted to do was give her lice. I had to make the phone call. I could not believe it. We had just met them, and now I had to make THAT phone call. I was so humiliated.

I tried to handle the lice by myself. I went to the drug store and bought the chemicals and did the treatments. We had it pretty bad. I thought I had taken care of it. I could not have been more wrong—again. I went back to work, the kids went back to day care, and then the call came from the teachers again. Not over. She still had it. I had no idea. Talk about guilt. I was mortified and embarrased that I had no idea what to do.

> Always assume summer camps have the buggies and prepare accordingly. Braid hair and use prevention shampoo and spray and comb weekly just to be sure.

I scoured the internet and found a woman who was a registered nurse who would come to the house and get rid of lice naturally. She used conditioner, a comb, and her own chair and lamp. It was amazing. Unbelievably expensive, but out of desperation I would have given her the keys to my home if it meant I could get rid of the buggies; $500 later we were clean and she gave me the instructions to clean my house.

The next step was to wash everything, or put in dryer. All sheets, blankets, pillows, bed covers—everything. Remember, I had a baby and a three-year-old. We had a lot of soft, fluffy stuff around. All of it was bagged up. Couch and rugs were vacuumed. I was told to wash my pillow, and her pillow, or put them in dryer every day for the next ten days. I was so tired I just decided to wash my daughter's bed stuff. My husband and I just went without a comforter for ten days. It was the better option. He was not amused.

Two weeks later we were checked again and all clean.

We got the go ahead to unbag all the pillows and throw the blankets and stuffed toys we had put in bags in the basement. Considering we were hosting my family of thirty to forty people for our first Thanksgiving in the new house, a few days later, we needed to be buggie free.

At that point I had learned a lot. The first thing I learned is to ask for help. It was more than I could handle. Next big lesson was that those drug store chemicals do not work—especially when you have a bad case of it. I also learned lice do not jump or fly, they crawl—and crawl fast. They like clean hair, not dirty hair, and using tea tree oil and smelling hippie dippy may potentially prevent them, but is not a guarantee. Lastly, braids are the best defense. Keep hair up and tight and you will have less likelihood of getting them.

At the time, I created a spray of tea tree oil, water, lavender, and rosemary. I sprayed every day. We smelled pretty funky and hippie dippy, but I did not want to go through that again. I searched the market for a prevention spray, but nothing was available. A few years later there were a handful of companies making prevention kits. I guess I just missed my window to have my own "mommy invention."

After that, I thought I was an expert. Again—not so much. Every year the note comes home in the summer and the fall that there is lice in class, day care, or camp. It seems to be summer camps where it spreads like wildfire, and then that first week of September is the height of it. I was prepared. I would never let it happen again.

I was wrong.

We had a few bug-free years despite the notes that came home. Then it happened again. It was the day before school started. My kids were home with my husband while

I was at work. My neighbor called and left a message on my cell saying, "May not be important, I realize you are working but you may want to call me back."

Huh, that's weird. I was her house a few days earlier for a barbecue with our other neighbors who I had just met. There were six adults and eight kids between the families; seven boys and my daughter. I called her back, and she said that one of the boys in the other family had found one bug in her son's hair. It may be nothing, but I should check my kids. I hung up as fast as I could and started to look. My son had very short military haircut at the time and he looked fine to me. There was not much to check. My daughter—oh boy. It took a while, but I started to find bugs.

I immediately picked up the phone to call the nurse from a few years ago. She now owned a salon dedicated to lice removal. No joke, she has a bunch of girls working there, and she charges a fortune and is super busy. I got an appointment for later that night. As I was making the appointment my husband came downstairs with bags in hand and car service waiting to take him to the airport for a business trip. He saw I was a bit crazed, and said, "Good luck, see you Friday night—oh and happy birthday." Did I mention that Friday was my fortieth birthday? Happy Birthday to me, ugh!

I had just had my hair colored, so I figured I would be fine. I figured wrong. Yes, they don't like colored hair, but that does not stop them from laying eggs. My daughter had a lot. She needed to be fully deloused. My son had a bunch of babies and recently hatched nits. I missed it. Oh my— that's not good. I wound up having only one bug, but forty nits. Forty nits! That meant I had bugs that laid eggs and then those grew up and laid more. The coloring made them run from my head—most likely to my boy. What a shit show, to be frank. Hundreds of dollars later and exhausted, we were buggie free by about 10:30 p.m. I then took my newly clean children and self home and stripped beds so they could go to sleep. They got to bed before midnight. After all, the next day was the first day of school. I stayed up doing the rest of the cleaning, drying, bagging, and vacuuming until about two o'clock in the morning. See what happens when I drop the ball?

My husband returned home on my birthday and I made him sleep in the basement in case he had it. The next day he went in to the lice lady for a check. Nothing. What a relief, because we were now bug-free and only in follow-up phase. Follow-up is no joke, either. One time a week for the next two weeks they recommend soaking hair with Crisco. Yes, Crisco. Let it sit for at least six hours. I literally covered all of our heads, then put on old lady shower caps and went to bed. The next day, the only way to get it out was to use dish detergent. So glad I spent so much on hair color— right! I don't like to wash it after a color, let alone wash with dish detergent and soak with Crisco.

Don't panic, it is not dangerous. The bugs do not carry disease and they will not hurt you. It is an annoyance and hard for many people to deal with, but like anything else, it too will pass.

Here is a big lesson I learned. Crisco or olive oil are great treatments. If you suspect bugs, you can saturate hair with either and that will suffocate any bugs. If you do it every week for a few weeks the idea is it will take care of any bugs that hatch after treatment. Eggs hatch five to seven days after they are laid.

I am obviously pretty open to telling people if we have them. That is also so important. So often when people have lice they become embarrassed and ashamed and don't tell anyone. The problem is that the people they may have given it to, or even gotten it from, may not know they have it. If you are open to talking about lice, you may be able to slow the spread. I told all families we were in contact with because it is the right thing to do. Because of that, I have gotten calls from friends and neighbors asking me to "check" their kids because they have never had it and don't know what to look for, but someone they were in contact with has had them. My husband thinks that I should go into business doing lice checks. No thank you! Buggies still gross me out!

Since that episode a few years back we have had one or two times where we were in contact with them, but it hasn't gotten to the point of infesting the entire family. By combing weekly and checking with a flashlight as needed, I have learned to prevent it. We have had one or two instances where I found a bug or a nit in one of my children but I now know how to comb it out, use Crisco, and comb again. I can take care of it before it becomes a problem. I still like to pop into the lice treatment place for a check to be sure. Prevention spray is a part of the morning routine (when I remember).

Always assume summer camps have the buggies and prepare accordingly. Braid hair and use prevention shampoo and spray, and comb weekly just to be sure. This way if you do have something, you can find it and treat it before it spreads to others in the household. Checking weekly is the best way to prevent bigger issues. Take a comb on wet hair saturated with conditionerand not fully rinsed. Use the lice comb from the drug store. Wipe the comb on a white paper towel. If you have a problem, you will find it. It is better to do it wet, because flaky dry skin will come off on your comb if you do it dry. This can be confusing and and hard to differentiate bugs, nits, or just flakes of skin.

Don't panic, it is not dangerous. The bugs do not carry disease, and they will not hurt you. It is an annoyance and hard for many people to deal with, but like anything else, it too will pass. If you find yourself with the buggies, take a deep breath and know it is not your fault. We have all been there.

Time for Help:
The Sitter Dilemma

Who you let watch your baby is a huge decision, especially in the beginning. I know a lot of folks who will not let anyone but family watch their kids. No one. Ever. I also know families that hire a baby nurse at birth. Just as with every parenting decision, it is personal and completely subjective. What is good for one family is not necessarily good for another. You have to decide what you are comfortable with. Also, what you are comfortable with changes over time. When I first returned to work, my father told me to work to not make any drastic changes for the first six months. He was right. I had moments of panic in the beginning, questioning my decision to return to work. In the long run I am so happy with the decisions I made for me, however my decisions are not right for everyone.

The first time my husband and I left our baby with grandma and grandpa we went to dinner (early bird, of course). I was not feeling myself since giving birth, and my daughter was only a few weeks old. By the way, those mommies who walk out of the hospital after giving birth in their pre-pregnancy jeans, feeling good in heels on the way to a party—they exist—I have seen it—but I was not one of them. A month later my body was still foreign to me. If that is you, it's okay, it will eventually get better. I think I felt human again at about three to four months after delivery.

So, I went to dinner about twenty minutes from my parents' home and I worried the entire time. I know, I know, they raised me and my sister. God knows I was reminded of that constantly, but that did not ease my stress level. I was a brand-new, neurotic, and anxious, mom. Well, the baby survived, and so did I.

When you are a bit of a control freak, childcare options can be challenging. Over time I got used to the idea of hiring sitters other than family. Day care teachers are awesome choices, as well as teenagers living in your neighborhood. I have tried agencies as well as referrals from friends. Overall I have had mixed results. You need to use your gut and ask a lot of questions. I had an excellent college student from New York City when I lived in Jersey City. She had a ton of younger cousins and spent her entire teen years babysitting back home. Now in the City going to school, she would hop on the PATH train and come over. The only downside was that if we wanted to stay out later than the PATH ran, we would have to drive her home. My husband and I took turns driving her back to Manhattan.

I want to bring up the elephant in the room when women start the search for a nanny or sitter. Will she be too pretty? Some of you may be thinking that is such a silly or superficial thought. However, so many women I know seem to have it, that I felt it important to mention. I know I thought it! After having a baby, the confident, sexy mojo is not exactly in full gear for many of us. Hiring a young attractive woman does not make it better. I had a relative once say to me that she could not believe I let my husband drive our nineteen-year-old sitter home in the middle of the night. As funny as the comment seemed, I get it. Unfortunately, so many of us have insecurities about our attractiveness as we become moms, and as we age. The best advice I can provide here is to put things into perspective. There will be things in your life you cannot control. Base your choices on sitters on how they take care of your kids. One of the fastest ways to feel bad about yourself is to compare yourself to others. Don't do it. Your relationship with your husband is your relationship, and having a pretty nanny should not change that. I have a few friends who have had "hot nannies." I remember one who was from Brazil and wore a midriff shirt to my friend's son's third birthday party. OMG! I thought every dad in the room was going to have a heart attack when she walked into the room. It is easier to say than to know, but remember if you are secure in yourself and your relationship it shouldn't matter. Despite knowing this, you do not need to feel ashamed or embarrased for thinking it. Many of us do too. Just remember the confident, beautiful woman you are!

One important lesson I learned when searching for sitters was to find someone my kids want to be around. Younger sitters are great because they are more like playmates. That works better as your baby gets past the toddler stage. I also learned that younger sitters can be less expensive. When you factor in the cost of a movie and dinner, price matters. The most important thing I learned was to HAVE SOMEONE. Time with your spouse is crucial, and as moms, we often put our kids first and our relationship with our spouse second. That can create issues in the long run.

Kids thrive when parents are happy. Parents need time together away from the kids. Kids benefit from being with sitters. They learn that it's okay when mommy and daddy go out and that they always come back home. It helps them develop independence. From a parent's perspective, until I had children I never knew how much of a luxury it was to have a waiter bring me a meal and not hear "I need to go potty" the moment the food was placed in front of me. Eating my meal while still warm was suddenly a treat! Another tip I have is to find friends that you are comfortable with taking your kids overnight, and visa versa. You can trade off and get a night alone, and then you return the favor and take their kids. It is cheaper and the kids look at it as a treat, not realizing it is a treat for mommy and daddy, too. Recently, our kids had a sleepover, and instead of going out we stayed home and watched the movie *Ted* and ate a box of Oreos. Pretty perfect evening!

> Kids thrive when parents are happy.

Learning to not feel guilty about taking time for myself is a work in progress. I catch myself not wanting to leave my kids. Especially overnight. Whether it comes from the years of traveling for business, or just plain control issues, I believe it is important to take some time for you and your spouse. Some days it is easier than others.

One funny story, a few years ago I had my daughter in gymnastics at a local gym that offered a parents' night babysitting. I had credit from missed classes and could bring both my kids for free. Why not? What I did not know was that all of the other kids were toddlers. Mine were seven and ten at the time. When I picked them up after dinner my oldest pulled me aside and whispered in my ear, "Mom, did you like dinner? I hope so because you owe me. I had to sing "Wheels on the Bus."" Oops. I am glad she was a good sport about it.

Then there's the full-day sitter dilemma. If you are going back to work, do you go with day care or nanny? That is always a tough decision. I know lots of folks who are happy with both. I chose day care. Here was my reasoning: If my child did not bond, or was not treated exactly as I wanted by one person, there were other teachers or staff in the room. I was not putting care into one person's hands. Day care has a checks and balance system. It worked for me. It gave me comfort.

That very first day back to work with my first child was not easy. I remember hanging around and chatting with another mom, and I asked how she was handling this whole day care thing. She responded with, "I did not get my MBA to sit around and fingerpaint all day. That's what day care is for."

I thought, "Wow! I like this woman." Now I may not agree totally, but it was just a relief to know that I was not alone in my desire to go to work and the fact that on some level I did not think I could be happy at home all day playing with a baby or toddler. That helped a lot.

There can be a tremendous amount of mommy guilt and I would love to tell you that you won't feel it, but no matter how sure you are about your choice, it is normal to feel uncertain. It gets better. Know your own limits and what makes you feel more confident as a mom. Also keep in mind that any decision you make is a decision for the time being. It does not need to be forever. Circumstances can change and so can your childcare decision.

As children get older, working moms are faced with what to do in the summer. Summer camp can be challenging for working and non-working moms, alike. I actually found when I worked full-time, that summer was easier. I found a great camp that ran from eight thirty in the morning until five thirty in the afternoon every day. And the kids loved it. They came home exhausted and filthy, exactly what I wanted to see. I felt bad that we did not have much of a choice, but the kids really loved going. At the time, I knew rationally how great this camp was, and how much they enjoyed it, and yet I was filled with guilt over the fact that there was not a lot of choice.

The ability for my kids to be on the swim team or hang out at the pool or playground with mom, like I did as a child, was not an option at the time. Years later when I had the ability to work less in the summer, I asked my daughter about swim team and she said, "No, mom, that's your thing, I don't like swimming that much."

All that time I felt bad that I was not able to give her opportunities I had and she did not even want them. That's pretty much how it goes. So much of what we moms stress about and feel guilty over are things we create in our own minds. Often far from the reality.

As I started my own counseling practice, I wanted to spend more time with them, so the first summer I limited my work hours to two days a week and spent three days a week mostly with the kids. That worked out fairly well, however it was hard to find a camp for two days a week. Even if you are home summers, it can be boring for the kids. By the following year I learned having half day structured activities and afternoons to hang out worked the best for us.

There were times that I felt guilty about leaving my children with others, but looking back, it was unnecessary guilt. For example, at around nine months old my daughter would stand holding the day care teacher's hand as the teacher sang "Ring around the Rosy." At the end my baby would say "dooah." OMG, she said down. I was so jealous.

When I sang "Ring around the Rosy" I got nothing. I even tried it with a Spanish accent to sound like her teacher. Silly yes, but I was a desperate mom. Looking back I am so grateful for the time she had with her teachers, and the love they gave her. My jealousy was a product of my own creation. When you are at work or away from your kids, trust you made a good decision and your baby is fine. When you are with your baby or your family, leave work alone. Don't multi-task. It doesn't work. Be mindful of the moment you are in and you will save a lot of mommy guilt later.

Dressing:
The Five-Year-Old Fashionista

When I first learned we were having a baby girl, I found myself in the children's section of the department store picturing our little bundle of joy in adorable outfits. That's not exactly how it turned out.

Baby pastel pink took over every gift at my baby shower. I think I had seven fluffy pink zip-up newborn snowsuits, many of them with little bunny ears or something cutsie on top. I never used any of them—the car seat blanket zipped in and out and other than a hat and blankets, I never had a use for any of the infant snowsuits. I learned quickly that coats are not necessary for a winter baby.

Those expensive newborn outfits look nice when you first put them on, however after about a minute they become covered in spit up, drool, or poop. Newborn clothes need to be changed often. Be prepared to do a lot of laundry. If you spend a ton of money on designer clothes you will be quickly disapointed as they quickly become stained. I learned to buy lots of inexpensive basics that are easy to take on and off.

You will also find yourself with gifts of clothing that you don't particularly like. Know that is only the beginning. One tip is to keep track of who gave you what outfit, and try to put the baby in that outfit when you see the person who gave it to you. Trust me, it is much easier that way. Eventually you will lose the ability to have full control over how he or she looks anyway, so get over it early. Once my daughter was about eighteen months old I heard "I do it" every time we got dressed. She insisted on choosing what to wear. The control freak in me did not like it, but I learned to get over it. There was a phase around that time where EVERY day was a skirt or dress. The idea of pants or leggings or anything on her legs put her into an unbelievable meltdown.

Some kids have strong opinions about what they put on every day. They have so little control over what they eat, what they do in school, when they play, and when they go places, that picking out clothes is a way for them to have some control over their environment and make their own choices. What they wear can give them a sense of power. To a young child, outfits are cool and they represent individuality—even if mommy thinks they look ridiculous. After all, look back at your pictures as a young kid. Many of them look pretty silly, I am sure. I often cringed at the choices my kids made in the morning, however I learned to let it go, and that I was not going to be doomed socially because of how my child looked when he or she left the house. Granted, some may criticize or raise an eyebrow, but overall does that really matter?

Mismatched clothing, bright colors, lots of dresses, and sparkles, and crazy jewelry were a daily experience for my daughter. I thought perhaps it was only a girl thing. Nope. My son is the same. Bright green sneakers, glow in the dark orange shirts with red shorts. He loves to stand out. I tried to explain the concept of clothes that "go," even if they don't "match." It was lost on my boy. His father always says to him "boys don't match," and he proves that every day.

My rule is, as long as they are appropriately dressed for the weather and not too "hoochy," just let it go.

The weather is another story all together. For some reason, boys seem to be obsessed with shorts in winter. I think it's about the fancy basketball socks they want to show off. Coldest and snowiest winter I have ever seen and my son wants to wear shorts and basketball sneakers every day.

One day my son wore sweatpants with his basketball sneakers to school on a very snowy cold day. He loved those bright orange basketball sneakers. I explained that the ground was full of snow and that he needed to wear snow boots and carry sneakers in his back pack. No deal. He was not having it.

Some kids have strong opinions about what they wear. They have so little control over what they eat, what they do in school, when they play, and when they go places, that picking out clothes is a way for them to have some control over their environment and make their own choices.

I am a huge believer that consequences should be felt by kids (within reason). It would not kill him to get wet feet. When he refused to listen I said, "Fine, you can go to school with your sneakers, but you will get wet and cold if you go in the snow." Well, what do you know? He played in the snow and in some puddles on the blacktop and after recess he had wet shoes, socks, and wet pants to his knees.

I got the call from the school nurse asking me to bring him new shoes, socks and pants.

I said, "No. He was aware of the consequences." I sensed that was not what she wanted to hear. After some back and forth, I reluctantly gave in. His feet were cold and she was concerned. I brought dry clothes to school and made sure that those basketball shoes he loves so much were put away until the spring. Later that day the office called to say he needed his sneakers for gym class since I brought him snow boots. Oh well. He missed gym class. Consequences are an important part of learning. If we do everything for our kids they won't learn how to make better choices for themselves. I still wish I had not gone in the first time to bring clothes in the first place.

One particular winter, all the boys wore shorts to school, even in the freezing cold. We finally made a rule that 20 degrees was our cut-off. If it was 20 degrees or above he could wear shorts, but under 20 degrees, he needed to wear long pants. Jackets too. Forget it, my son wore a zip-up fleece all winter long. So many mornings I was freezing in my heavy coat watching my little boy in shorts and fleece head off to school. I wondered if I was making a mistake letting him go to school like that, and felt guilty he might get sick. He did not get sick and when he felt cold he put on pants. Lessons are so much better learned through experience than through being forced by mom or dad. If there is one area where you are willing to loosen control early, I would suggest this one.

Hair is another way my kids like to assert independence. As early as I can remember, my girl wanted to do her own hair, and had a strong opinion on what it looked like. At age two she used to ask for "boo hair" which meant pig tails like the little girl in the movie

Monsters, Inc.

When she was ten-years-old I learned Kool Aid makes great hair dye. You would be surprised how many videos you can find on YouTube to learn how to dye hair with Kool Aid. Funny, Kool Aid was hard to find in my grocery store. I asked the man at the grocery store for Kool Aid and he looked at me like I was nuts. At that moment I quickly said that it wasn't to drink but to dye hair. As if that makes it better… ugh… that was clearly not my finest moment.

I know a lot of parents who have issues with colored hair, and I totally get it. My thought is this: Kids want to differentiate themselves (or to fit in with others). Either way they want to have control over an aspect of their appearance. Purple or red hair is just that: hair. I am okay with it. Hair can be cut. It is harmless. It isn't any different than my boy wanting to grow his long. I must say that bothers me more than my daughter wanting purple hair. Despite my personal opinion on what it looks like, I try not to say no for the sake of saying no. My kids don't want to dress or look like me, they want to be themselves. Once I accepted that fact, mornings became easier.

Teeth: Fear of the Dentist

The thought of going to a dentist brings up primal fears for many of us, my little ones included.

The question of when to take kids to see a dentist can lead to a variety of answers depending on who you ask. It is my understanding that if a baby has teeth, take him to check them out. That being said, we waited until age two. At that time we were told to get rid of the binky, hence the visit from the "binky fairy." Our binky fairy came to take all of our binkies to new babies and left us a stuffed toy. We still wound up at the orthodontist six years later, however it was a relief to be rid of the binky early on. Interestingly, having to search in unmentionable places to find a retainer for a tween isn't much different than searching for a binky for a toddler. I guess some things do not change over time.

One day we went as a family on a hike in the woods. We stopped at a clearing to sit on a tree stump and have snacks. My daughter had taken her retainer out of her mouth and put it in her lap, and of course forgot it was there as she got up to continue walking. As soon as we got home, she remembered her retainer. I did not want to drive back to the hiking trail and search for this thing for so many reasons. First of all, yuck! If we were able to find it, it would be covered in dirt. Second, I was tired, after all we had just finished hiking. Third, I thought this was a natural consequence to help her learn responsibility. When she was younger, if she left a toy somewhere we did not go back for it and she learned how to keep better track of her toys. This was different; I was going to have to pay for another retainer and take her back to the orthodontist for an extra visit. Nope, I did not want to deal, so we went back to the woods. Believe it or not, we found it in the dirt right by that stump where we had snacks. We cleaned it off and it was as good as new. That was easier than the time we dug through the public garbage can at Whole Foods for it.

> What they observe you doing is what they will ultimately do themselves.

Both of my kids had different experiences at the dentist. One was, and is still, traumatized and winds up with cavity after cavity, and the other has pretty uneventful visits. My son just the other day bit into a piece of candy and pulled out a silver cap for the second time! Either way, I would say to start as early as you can. Brushing teeth routinely and getting comfortable with dental visits will go smoother if it is introduced sooner rather than later. I know parents who still hover over their grammer school age kids to brush every day. I don't, but perhaps I should. I remind them at bedtime and ask them as I tuck them in if they brushed.

My son has admitted that he often says yes even if he did not do it. Most of the time I call his bluff and tell him to do it again, and send him to the bathroom. My daughter will say yes, but if she had not brushed, she will get up after I tuck her in to brush so as to not have lied about it.

If you can avoid the sugar drinks early, and have your children get used to water when transitioning from bottles, it will save you a lot of hassle later on as well. I have also found the more you have your little ones in the bathroom when you, yourself, brush, the more they want to do it, too. What they observe you doing is what they will ultimately do   themselves.

Listening Ears:
Will They Ever Learn to Listen?

I sometmes think the sound of my voice is just background noise for my kids. When they were toddlers we would say "open your listening ears," and expect kids to follow directions. Not quite that simple.

One day when my son was around two years old, he was playing with his toy cars in the family room by throwing them dangerously close to the TV. My husband, who was sitting three feet from him, repeatedly asked him to stop throwing the cars. He even raised his voice, which he hardly ever does. My husband then turned to me and said, "Do you think that he could have a problem with his hearing?" I thought about it for a brief second and from the other side of the room I whispered softly, "Who's momma's favorite little boy?" My boy jumped up and down raising his arms and said, "I am! I am! I am!" Silly Daddy, his hearing is just fine.

I learned when I say, "Stop blah blah blah" my kids hear "blah blah blah." Be affirmative, not negative. If you want your little one to stop running up and down the hallway you instinctively say, "Stop running down the hallway." Somehow your child misses the "stop" part and hears "run down the hallway." Instead, try telling him or her to come to you, or put feet together. Always try to tell them what TO DO instead of what NOT TO DO. Seems subtle, but it can save you from more than a few angry escalations.

I repeat myself way more than I should. I know the importance of consequences, and follow through, and setting clear boundaries. I know what I am supposed to do. One of my first social work jobs was back in the late 1990's where I used to teach parenting skills classes to overwhelmed parents before I even had my own kids. It is so much easier to know what to do than to actually do it. Sometimes, I turn into the crazy screaming mommy I never wanted to become. Okay, more than sometimes. It is a work in progress, for sure.

Through my experiences and those of others, I have come to understand that most of us mommies and daddies yell at our children. We know it is not ideal, and find ourselves feeling guilty afterwards. We understand the need to set better boundaries and follow through with consequences, and yet we get derailed. Funny, how we find ourselves trying to regain control of our kids by being insanely out of control. Using time out can help mommies as much as it helps kids. Stepping away (often in the bathroom) long enough to count to ten and breathe before returning to deal with the situation can make a huge difference.

Your kids will test limits and piss you off. It happens. It's normal. Give yourself a break—it's not the first time or the last time you will not be perfect. Parenting is a learning experience for mommy as well as for the child. They will be okay.

I have learned that if I screw up, I need to acknowledge it to myself and to my kids. Apologize, if need be, is in of itself is a good lesson for the children. Talk with them about how mommy sometimes makes mistakes, and what mommy could have done differently. Show them that even when you are as old as dirt you still have things to learn, and that is okay. They key is to make meaningful change moving forward. As they grow, we as parents grow, too. Kids will have a hard time learning to control themselves if we as parents are not in control of our reaction to them acting out. It starts with us. It is amazing the changes I see in my children when I am able to better control my temper and follow-through on consequences as needed.

Start by recognizing that parenting can be hard, but you can absolutely handle it. Learning self-control and mindfulness meditation has helped me yell less often. By better understanding myself and what my triggers are, I can better self-regulate. Stop and pause when you can, and take a moment to breathe while you think through your response before you make it. Letting older kids know that is what you are doing also models behaviors you want to see in them as well.

Most of us mommies and daddies yell at our children. We know it is not ideal and find ourselves feeling guilty afterwards. We understand the need to set better boundaries and follow through with consequences, and yet we get derailed.

I have begun using mind-fulness exercises in my therapy practice and continue to learn more and more as I practice. Previously, I was intimidated by the idea of meditating, and used to think it was not for me. I was never good at sitting still. I equated "busy" with "good." The busier I was, the better. I had not really seen the benefit of slowing down. I did not think I had the luxury to slow down, either. Just like anything else we want for ourselves, we can make the time if it is important and we see the value of it. After all, I certainly had the time to get to Level 300 on Candy Crush, so how could I not add an extra few minutes a day to do something that will improve my overall health and well-being?

Once I made the decision I needed to create a routine for myself that worked. After trial and error I found using simple guided meditations from various phone apps or YouTube videos was the right fit for me. It takes less than twenty minutes a day. I have even introduced the concept to my children, and found a few kid-friendly age-appropriate meditation practices we have done together. I have noticed that when they see me using breathing techniques when I am upset or overwhelmed they are more likely to try it themselves.

Putting labels on our feelings also helps, as well. We use the term "ugly monster" when we have tantrums.

> I was never good at sitting still. I equated "busy" with "good." The busier I was the better. I had not really seen the benefit of slowing down.

When my kids were in preschool, we started having conversations about feelings and what happens when we are angry or upset or feel hurt. Sometimes we can lose control of our emotions and that is when the ugly monster can take over. We talk about ways to prevent the ugly monster by using breathing exercises to help us feel more in control when we are upset. The favorite and easiest one we use is counting candles. We close our eyes and imaging a beautiful candle in front of us and take a deep breath and then blow the air out and imagine blowing out the candle. We do this ten times and count each one. When tantrums begin to escalate we do the candles exercise slowly as many times as it takes to be able to then deal with whatever started the escalation in the first place. One time my son and I witnessed an argument in public by two teenagers and my son turned to me and said, "He needs to blow out some candles."

Another lesson I learned through trial and error (and more error) is to keep directions short. If I lecture my kids to do something like putting shoes away they often don't do it. However if I point and say "shoes, now" they get it. The less words, the more they hear.

The last and most important lesson I learned is to make consequences as natural as possible. Punishment should fit the crime. For example, my kids are always leaving stuff around the house and not putting them away. Especially the electronic devices and games. When I see that they have been left on the couch and are almost out of battery I do not put the items on the chargers for them. I let them run out of power and when they go to play a game and the device is dead, they learn to charge it next time. It does not always work but it is more effective than nagging.

There seems to be a culture of coddling kids more than I believe is necessary. When your little ones start to pass toddlerhood I guarantee they will be capable of doing more than you think. Don't fall into the trap of doing everything for them. Teaching them to take on age-appropriate responsibilities will go a long way to teaching them life skills. Your seven-year-old is fully able to vacuum or set the table. Kids can help cook and fold laundry with you as they get old enough. Encourage them to take responsibility.

They can put their own clothes away. Sometimes you need to come up with ways to make it easier for them to reach things, but they can be learn to help out around the house. We use a system of stickers for doing chores and pay out 50 cents per sticker. They earn a few dollars here and there, and it teaches them responsibility. There is no reason kids cannot empty backpacks after school, starting in kindergarten, and help pack lunches for the next day.

In our house, if they forget lunch or forget something for school, I will come and bring it to them one time. I will come and drop off the lunch or the flute or whatever they forgot, one time each school year. After that they go without. They will not starve to death without a snack and will deal with missing gym if they go to school with no sneakers or sit out of music class with no instrument. It may sound a little harsh to some, however I believe it has a stronger and more meaningful impact.

Following through on consequences is not easy by any means. Just recently my son (at age seven) was at a pool with friends. After he came home I took my two kids to our pool club. He said he did not want to swim any more that day and chose not to wear his bathing suit. I told him to put on his bathing suit. He refused. I told him to pack his suit in case he needed it. I could have packed it myself, but I didn't. I told him to do it. He didn't. Sure enough, he got to pool and wanted to swim. He asked me to go home to get it. I said no. He had a major meltdown tantrum in public. Crap. I hate those public meltdowns. It feels as if every single person in the tri-state area is watching my kid behave like an ass and thinking, "What a horrible parent."

The reality is, most parents watching feel bad for you because they have been there, too. Some will judge you, as I am sure some did judge me that day, but that really shouldn't be my concern. My focus needed to be on my son. I did my best to reiterate to him that he was told to bring a suit, and we were going home in two hours. I gave him a choice to go on the playground or go swimming in the pool in his clothes. He refused, and continued to yell and cry. It would have been so easy to just scoop him up and bring him home to change, but I knew that short-term solution would not be good for him, or me, in the long-term. I did my best to not react. I wanted to react—a lot. Eventually he got tired of yelling and calmed down. After a while he got up and went in the pool in his clothes. Problem solved.

Public meltdowns can take a big toll on parents. It is one thing to have your child test limits at home, but when it happens in front of the world, a whole new level of emotions kicks in. Not only defiance, but any type of public meltdown can be challenging. It is easy to witness a child having a meltdown in public and judge the parent. We have all seen it, at the grocery store or the mall, a child is yelling or not listening, and as observers we think we would handle it better. Before being a mom I had those very same thoughts. Now I know better. It happens to all of us, and in that moment it helps to know we are not alone. A smile and a quick, "I've been there" can go a long way to helping another mom or dad deal with difficult parenting moments. Resist the urge to judge or give advice in the moment.

> Sometimes we can lose control of our emotions and that is when the ugly monster can take over. We talk about ways to prevent the ugly monster by using breathing exercises to help us feel more in control when we are upset.

Speaking of public meltdowns, recently my family and I were on vacation at a water park. I should probably preface this story with the fact that I am not a fan of scary rides or heights at all. In fact, I almost never go on any rides with the kids. I always hold the stuff and let my husband do the scary stuff. This day, my husband and daughter ran right for the biggest slides and were super excited to go on them. I was not thrilled, and neither was my son. He refused to go on anything and said it was too high up. He was old enough and tall enough and I knew he would enjoy it. My husband tried to drag him up the stairs but that did not work, he was too anxious. My son began to panic and cry even more.

That's when good intentioned strangers stepped in. As much as they tried to help, they were having the opposite effect. The more they tried to convince him, the more frightened he became. At that moment we created SAM. SAM stood for "scary ass monster" and SAM was trying to protect my son from getting hurt. I explained to him that SAM sometimes shows up to protect us, even when we don't need him. He wants to keep us safe and sometimes he goes a little overboard. Together we asked SAM to let us walk just to the next landing and then we would re-evaluate the situation. We did this several times with each landing and eventually made it to the top of the slide. The entire time we were met with lots of strangers who provided advice on how we "should" handle the situation. In the end my son not only went down the slide but he had a blast the rest of the day going up and down just about every slide at the park.

It is amazing how much unsolicited advice you will get when out in public with your kids. Don't let it get you flustered. Everyone has an opinion on what you should do, especially when your child is misbehaving, or just plain freaking out. Don't let it overwhelm you. You are doing fine!

We all want to be the best parents we can possibly be. We seek an unattainable ideal and beat ourselves up emotionally when we make mistakes. Mistakes will happen, you are human. The great news is your children are human, too. Teaching them to love and respect themselves starts with us. If we can grow and learn to let go of perfection, we will be more resilient and foster that same resiliency and kindness in our children. It starts with letting go of the guilt, being kind to yourself and knowing YOU GOT THIS!

Siblings: Or Frenemies?

My baby sister is one of my best friends and someone I admire very much. She and her husband even moved in with us temporarily a few years ago. It was supposed to be a few weeks, but turned into a few months. I was so happy to have her around all the time. My husband and her husband did not share the joy. They get along great, but I am sure each of them wanted their privacy back quickly.

When we were kids it was a different story between us. We fought with each other as many siblings do. Sibling rivalry is something I know is normal, and yet sometimes I look at my children and think that all they do is fight with each other.

The typical scenario in my house is the little one bothers the big one and the big one bosses around the little one. My son treats annoying his sister as a sport—and he's good at it. She cannot let it go without getting back at him. As much as they argue, they also have loving and caring moments that make my heart melt.

Kids will learn how to interact with each other from how they see parents and adults in their life treating each other. My husband and I do not fight very often. When we do, we try not to do it in front of the kids, but sometimes it happens.

I think we keep it appropriate, but I can tell when we

bicker in front of them, that they react to it. Not just mommy and daddy, but other relationships make an impact as well.

When my daughter was three years old, I was bickering with my mother in front of her. My daughter was sitting on top of the kitchen table and waved me to come closer. She whispered in my ear, "Mommy, you know better." That was a huge defining moment for me and really made me see how much my behavior affects her.

I think about that moment in times when I get frustrated or find myself not being as good a role model as I could be. The lesson I learned that day is that kids will watch everything. Telling them to get along with each other is not as powerful as modeling how to get along with others.

> My son treats annoying his sister as a sport—and he's good at it. She cannot let it go without getting back at him. As much as they argue, they also have loving and caring moments that make my heart melt.

I also learned to not get too upset when they argue, but to help them to work things out between them the best they can. One very common argument we had for a while was how to play together when it was just the two of them. My son wants to play video games and sports. My daughter wants to play school and paint nails. I pride myself on encouraging gender neutral activities, however things do not always work out that way.

If I leave it to them to work things out, instead of doing it for them they usually come up with a good plan where they take turns picking activities. Getting out and shooting hoops or painting toe nails works for both of them.

Don't feed into mommy guilt when your kids bicker with each other, it is normal and natural. Eventually they will mature, and so will their relationship. No matter who comes in and out of their world, they will always have each other.

Kick Ass Mom: Don't Forget It!

Whether or not you are reading this as a mom frustrated with mommy guilt and looking to know you are not alone, or you are expecting or planning to start a family, know that you are, and will, be a fantastic mom! You are the center of the universe to your little one, and have a wonderful opportunity to learn and grow right alongside of your baby. Throughout my journey so far I have learned many lessons through trial and error, and more error. I yell, I cry, I feel guilty, and I forgive.

Parenting is hard. It's not glamorous and often seems beyond overwhelming. I have made a lot of mistakes and will continue to do so, however I have learned to not let mommy guilt take over. Being a wife and a mom are the greatest achievements of my life. I am so very proud of my children and myself each and every day. My kids are happy, healthy, and human. As a mom, I love them and love myself. Your journey as a mom will be filled with mistakes, forgiveness, and love. Forget that mommy guilt and know you got this!

About The Author

Cara Maksimow is a clinical therapist, coach, speaker, wife and mom living in Northern NJ. She has her undergraduate degree in Psychology from Rutgers University, her MSW from Columbia University Graduate School of Social Work, and a Certificate in Professional Coaching. Since 2014 she has owned Maximize Wellness Counseling and Coaching, LLC, where she provides supportive counseling for people navigating through times of transition, stress, anxiety and depression. She works collaboratively with her clients to identify strengths, problem solve, reach goals and increase resiliency. Prior to starting her practice, she spent thirteen years working for a pharmaceutical company as a trainer and sales manager.

She and her husband both grew up in the same town in northern NJ. They began dating at their ten-year high school reunion, married shortly after, and have two amazing children who are now transitioning into adolescents. Cara loves to spend her free time reading psychology books, binge-watching Netflix, and hanging out with her family and friends. She believes her greatest achievement is raising her children to be kind and happy despite all of her mistakes along the way.

32908847R00085

Made in the USA
Middletown, DE
22 June 2016